CAMBRIDGE LIBRARY COLLECTION

Books of enduring scholarly value

Literary Studies

This series provides a high-quality selection of early printings of literary works, textual editions, anthologies and literary criticism which are of lasting scholarly interest. Ranging from Old English to Shakespeare to early twentieth-century work from around the world, these books offer a valuable resource for scholars in reception history, textual editing, and literary studies.

A Jane Austen Dictionary

The novels of Jane Austen (1775–1817) are of remarkable and enduring appeal; popular the world over, they are celebrated for their wit and social observation. This 1932 publication was compiled by George Latimer Apperson (1857–1937), an inspector of schools, editor of *The Antiquary* from 1899 to 1915, and major contributor to the *Oxford English Dictionary*. His stated intention for this work was to 'include in one alphabet, the name of every person, place, book and author named in Jane Austen's novels, fragments and juvenilia'. He also extends his coverage to biographical detail, drawing on the landmark study *Jane Austen: Her Life and Letters* (1913). The dictionary was published at a time when Jane Austen scholarship and literary criticism had developed significantly, reflecting the continued public interest in her novels. It remains an indispensable reference tool for all admirers of her work.

T0345348

Cambridge University Press has long been a pioneer in the reissuing of out-of-print titles from its own backlist, producing digital reprints of books that are still sought after by scholars and students but could not be reprinted economically using traditional technology. The Cambridge Library Collection extends this activity to a wider range of books which are still of importance to researchers and professionals, either for the source material they contain, or as landmarks in the history of their academic discipline.

Drawing from the world-renowned collections in the Cambridge University Library and other partner libraries, and guided by the advice of experts in each subject area, Cambridge University Press is using state-of-the-art scanning machines in its own Printing House to capture the content of each book selected for inclusion. The files are processed to give a consistently clear, crisp image, and the books finished to the high quality standard for which the Press is recognised around the world. The latest print-on-demand technology ensures that the books will remain available indefinitely, and that orders for single or multiple copies can quickly be supplied.

The Cambridge Library Collection brings back to life books of enduring scholarly value (including out-of-copyright works originally issued by other publishers) across a wide range of disciplines in the humanities and social sciences and in science and technology.

A Jane Austen Dictionary

GEORGE LATIMER APPERSON

CAMBRIDGE
UNIVERSITY PRESS

CAMBRIDGE
UNIVERSITY PRESS

University Printing House, Cambridge, CB2 8BS, United Kingdom

Cambridge University Press is part of the University of Cambridge.

It furthers the University's mission by disseminating knowledge in the pursuit of
education, learning and research at the highest international levels of excellence.

www.cambridge.org
Information on this title: www.cambridge.org/9781108082358

© in this compilation Cambridge University Press 2015

This edition first published 1932
This digitally printed version 2015

ISBN 978-1-108-08235-8 Paperback

A JANE AUSTEN
DICTIONARY

A JANE AUSTEN DICTIONARY

BY

G. L. APPERSON, I.S.O.

Author of *English Proverbs and Proverbial Phrases,*
The Social History of Smoking, etc.

CECIL PALMER
FORTY-NINE
CHANDOS
STREET
W.C.2

F I R S T
E D I T I O N
1 · 9 3 2
COPYRIGHT

Made and Printed in Great Britain at the Kemp Hall Press Ltd
in the City of Oxford

TO
THE LOVED MEMORY
OF
JANE AUSTEN

PREFATORY NOTE

IN compiling this Dictionary it has been my aim to include in one alphabet :—

I. The name of every person, place, book, and author named in Jane Austen's (1) novels ; (2) fragments and Juvenilia :

II. The titles of all her works, with brief particulars of composition and publication ;

III. (1) The names of the novelist, her parents, family, and near relations and connexions, with brief biographical details ; (2) the names of persons associated with her, and of places and localities inhabited or visited by her.

Under I-II the books dealt with are *Sense and Sensibility, Pride and Prejudice, Mansfield Park, Emma, Northanger Abbey, Persuasion, Lady Susan, Sanditon, The Watsons,* and *Love and Freindship* (including "Lesley Castle," "History of England," "A Collection of Letters," and "Scraps").

One chapter reference after a personal name indicates the first mention or appearance of the character in the story. When this reference is to a mention only, a second reference indicates the first actual appearance of the character on the scene. Occasionally a second reference is given for the sake of an apt descriptive quotation. The reference after a place name is to the first mention of that place in the story.

vii

With regard to III, the references are to the *Memoir*, by J. E. Austen-Leigh, second edition, 1871 ; the *Life and Letters*, by W. Austen-Leigh and R. A. Austen-Leigh, 1913 ; and the *Letters*, edited by Lord Brabourne, 2 vols., 1884.

Under both I and III references to localities in Bath and London are collected under the headings **Bath** and **London**, with cross references from the names of the various localities.

Illustrative quotations and notes are freely supplied throughout.

G.L.A.

Amersham.

ABBREVIATIONS

b, born.

C., Cassandra Austen.

" C. of L.," " A Collection of Letters," in *Love and Freindship*.

d., died.

E., *Emma*.

" H. of E.," " History of England," in *Love and Freindship*.

J. and J.A., Jane Austen.

Lady S., *Lady Susan.*

L. and F., *Love and Freindship.*

" Les. C.," " Lesley Castle," in *Love and Freindship*.

Lett., *Letters*, edited by Lord Brabourne, 2 vols., 1884.

Life, *Life and Letters*, by W. and R. A. Austen-Leigh, 1913.

m., married.

Mem., *Memoir*, by J. E. Austen-Leigh, 2nd edition, 1871.

M.P., *Mansfield Park.*

N.A., *Northanger Abbey.*

Pers., *Persuasion.*

P.P., *Pride and Prejudice.*

Sand., *Sanditon.*

S.S., *Sense and Sensibility.*

REFERENCES

THE references to the novels, *Sanditon* and the *Memoir* are to chapter; to *Lady Susan*, to Letter; to the *Life and Letters* and to the contents of *Love and Freindship*, to page; to *The Watsons* to page of the *Memoir*, 2nd edition, 1871; and to the *Letters*, 1884, to volume and page. The reference follows the quotation.

ACCIDENTALLY OMITTED.

Collins, William. Cousin to Mr. Bennet, and heir to his estate; rector of Hunsford, Kent. He was a tall, heavy-looking young man of five-and-twenty. His air was grave and stately, and his manners were very formal. *P.P.* xiii. Mr. Collins was not a sensible man, and the deficiency of nature had been but little assisted by education or society. *Ibid.* xv.

Collins, Mrs. *See* **Lucas, Charlotte.**

A

Abbeyland, The. We will walk to Sir John's new plantations at Barton Cross, and the Abbeyland. *S.S.*xlvi.

Abbey-Mill Farm, the home of the Martins. *E.*iv. .

Abbotts, The, pupils at Mrs. Goddard's school. The two
Abbotts and I ran into the front room and peeped
through the blind when we heard he was going by.
*E.*ix.

Abdy, John. Poor old man, he is bed-ridden . . . with the
rheumatic gout in his joints. *E.*xliv.

Abdy, John, junior. Head man at the Crown, ostler,
and everything of that sort. *E.*xliv.

Aberdeen, " Les. C." in *L. & F.* 47.

Address to Tobacco, by Isaac Hawkins Browne. *M.P.*
xvii. This was the " Pipe of Tobacco," published in
Dodsley's *Collection*.

" Adelaide and Theodore," by Madame de Genlis. *E.*liii.
The English translation was published in 1783.

Adlestrop Rectory was visited by Jane, with her sister
and mother, after their Bath home was broken up
in 1805.

Admiralty, The. *Pers.* viii.

"Adventures of Mr. Harley," an early sketch. *Life,* 57.

Agatha, a character in the play of *Lovers' Vows* (*q.v.*).
*M.P.*xiii.

Agatha. *See* **St. Clair.**

Agincourt, Battle of. " H. of E." in *L. & F.* 85.

Agricola. *N.A.*xiv.

Agricultural Reports, The, read by Robert Martin. *E.*iv.

Albion Place, Ramsgate. *M.P.*v.

Alfred the Great. *N.A.*xiv.

Alice, perhaps Miss Tilney's maid. *N.A.*xxviii.

Alicia, Lady. I was looking after some window-curtains,
which Lady Alicia and Mrs. Frankland were telling me
of last night. *Pers.* xix.

Allen, Mr.—who owned the chief of the property about
Fullerton, the village in Wiltshire where the Morlands
lived. *N.A.*i.

Allen, Mrs. Mrs. Allen was one of that numerous class
of females, whose society can raise no other emotion
than surprise at there being any man in the world who
could like them well enough to marry them. She had
neither beauty, genius, accomplishment, nor manner.
*N.A.*ii.

Allenham, Devon. The narrow winding valley of
Allenham. *S.S.*ix.

Allenham Court, the residence of Mrs. Smith, visited by
Willoughby. *S.S.*ix.

Almane, La Baronne d', in Mme de Genlis' *Adelaide
and Theodore.* *E.*liii.

Alps, The. *N.A.*xxv.

Alton, Hants, to which J. walked in 1813 (*Life* 260). She visited there in 1816 (*Life* 375). She must have been often there on other occasions.

Amelia, a character in *Lovers' Vows* (*q.v.*). *M.P.*xiv.

America. " C. of E." in *L. & F.* 108.

Anderson, Charles and **Miss Anderson.** The Andersons of Baker Street. *M.P.*v.

Andrew, Old, a gardener. *Sand.* iv.

Andrews, Miss, a friend of Isabella Thorpe. *N.A.*vi.

Anhalt, a character in *Lovers' Vows* (*q.v.*). *M.P.*xiv.

Anne of Denmark. " H. of E." in *L. & F.* 94.

Annersley, Admiral. " C of L." in *L. & F.* 107.

Annesley, Mrs., companion, to Georgiana Darcy—a genteel, agreeable-looking woman. *P.P.*xlv.

Antigua. Sir Thomas's means will be rather straitened if the Antigua estate is to make such poor returns. *M.P.*iii.

" Antwerp," The, William Price's ship. *M.P.*xi.

Arabella. " Scraps " in *L. & F.* 140.

Argyle Buildings. *See* **Bath.**

Ashburnham, Mr. and **Ashburnham,** his house. "C. of L." *in L. & F.* 109, 111.

Ashe, a parish adjoining Steventon, of which Mr. Lefroy was rector.

Ashe Park, the seat of the Holders, near Steventon. Often visited by J., e.g. *Lett.* i, 273.

Ashford, Kent, where J. attended a ball in 1798 (*Life,* 109).

Ashworth, near Longbourn. *P.P.*l.

Asia Minor. My cousin . . . never heard of Asia Minor. *M.P.*ii.

"Asp," The, the first ship commanded by Captain Wentworth. *Pers.* viii.

Astley's Circus. *See* **London.**

Atkinson, Miss. *Pers.* xix.

Atlantic, The. (1) *M.P.* xxiii. (2) Mrs. Croft says, " I have crossed the Atlantic four times." *Pers.* viii.

Augusta, sister to Margaret. " C. of L." in *L. & F.* 103.

Augusta. *See* **Lindsay.**

Augustus. Edward's most particular friend. *L. & F.* 15

Austen, Anna (1), *née* Mathew. *See* **Austen, James.**

Austen, Anne (2) *b.* April, 1793 : daughter of James Austen by his first wife : *m.* Ben Lefroy, November, 1814 : *d.* 1872.

Austen, Caroline, daughter of James Austen by his second wife. She assisted her brother, James Edward Austen-Leigh, in the preparation of the *Memoir.* She died unmarried in 1881.

Austen, Cassandra (1), *née* Leigh (*q.v.*) Jane's mother. She died and was buried at Chawton in January, 1827, aged 88.

Austen, Cassandra (2), the fifth child of George and Cassandra Austen, and elder sister of Jane, *b.* January, 1773. She became engaged to a young clergyman,

Thomas Fowle (*q.v.*), who accompanied a friend and kinsman (Lord Craven) to the West Indies, as chaplain to his regiment, and there died of yellow fever, 1797. Cassandra remained unmarried. She and Jane were devotedly attached to one another. It was the young Cassandra to whom the still more youthful Jane " inscribed with all due respect by the Author " her juvenile " History of England," printed in *Love and Freindship*. C. died in 1845 " at the house of her brother Francis, near Portsmouth—at his house, but in his absence." (*Life*, 402).

Austen, Charles, the eighth child of George and Cassandra Austen. *b.* June, 1779. Like his brother Francis he entered the navy and saw much active service. He rose to the rank of Admiral. Charles married twice : (1) in 1807, Fanny Palmer, of Bermuda ; (2) her sister, Harriet Palmer. By (1) he had three daughters, and by (2) two sons. He died of cholera (in a steam sloop on the Irrawaddy) in 1852, aged 73, being then in command of the East India and China station.

Austen, Edward, third son of George and Cassandra Austen. *b.* October 7, 1767. He was " early adopted by his cousin, Mr. Knight of Godmersham Park, in Kent, and Chawton House in Hampshire " (*Mem.*, i) properties which later (1797) came into Edward's possession. In November, 1812, Edward Austen took the name of Knight. In 1791 he married Elizabeth, daughter of Sir Brook Bridges, of Goodnestone, near Wingham, Kent, and settled for a time at Rowling, a small house near Goodnestone. " Some of Jane's earliest extant letters were written from Rowling "

(*Life*, 74). Edward and Elizabeth Austen had eleven children, the eldest being Fanny Catherine, *b*. January 23, 1793 (J.'s favourite niece), who *m*. Sir E. Knatchbull and became the mother of the Lord Brabourne who edited Jane Austen's *Letters*, 1884. Elizabeth Austen died in 1808, after the birth of her eleventh child. Edward Austen died in 1852.

Austen, Fanny Catherine, eldest daughter of Edward and Elizabeth Austen. *b*. January 23, 1793. She was the " My dear Niece " to whom Jane dedicated " my Opinions and Admonitions on the conduct of Young Women " (*L. & F.* 129). She married Sir Edward Knatchbull.

Austen, Francis, uncle of George Austen (1). He was " a successful lawyer at Tunbridge " (*Mem.* i). He provided for George Austen, orphaned at nine years old. His wife, Jane, was godmother to J.A.

Austen, Francis William, sixth child of George and Cassandra Austen. *b*. April, 1774. He entered the Royal Naval Academy in 1786, and went to sea two and a half years later. Like his brother Charles, he saw much active service, also rising to the rank of Admiral. He married twice : (1) in 1806 Mary Gibson ; (2) in 1828, Martha Lloyd. He had twelve children by the first wife. Francis died, aged 92, in 1865, G.C.B., and Senior Admiral of the Fleet.

Austen, George (1), the father of Jane—" of a family long established in the neighbourhood of Tenterden and Sevenoaks in Kent " (*Mem.* 1). He was educated at Tunbridge School and St. John's College, Oxford. He became Rector of Steventon in 1761, and of

Deane (in addition) in 1773. On April 26, 1764, he married Cassandra, youngest daughter of the Rev. Thomas Leigh, of the Warwickshire Leighs. They lived first at Deane, but in 1771 removed to Steventon. On his resignation of the livings of Steventon and Deane in 1801 they moved to Bath, where George Austen died January 21, 1805, and was buried at Walcot church.

Austen, George (2), second son of George and Cassandra Austen. *b.* August 26, 1766.

Austen, Henry, fourth child of George and Cassandra Austen. *b.* June, 1771. He followed various professions (*See Lett.* i, 33, 34), including that of banker, but became bankrupt early in 1816. Later in the same year he took orders. J. dedicated to him one of her juvenile productions, "Lesley Castle " (*L. & F.* 45). He contributed a short biographical notice of his sister to the first edition of her *Northanger Abbey* and *Persuasion*, published by John Murray in 1818. He married twice : (1) in December, 1797, his first cousin, Madame de Feuillide, *née* Hancock (*q.v.*), who died in 1813 ; (2) in 1820, Eleanor Jackson. There was no issue by either marriage. Henry Austen died at Tunbridge Wells in 1850.

Austen, James, first child of George and Cassandra Austen. *b.* February 13, 1765. He went to Oxford (St. John's) where " he obtained a ' founder's kin ' Scholarship, and, subsequently, a Fellowship " (*Life,* 46). James helped in the education of Jane and possibly contributed to the formation of her taste in literature. At Oxford, in 1789, " he became the

B

originator and chief author of a periodical paper called *The Loiterer* " (*Life*, 47). He took orders, and was first a curate at Overton, then at Deane, and later (in 1801) succeeded his father as Rector of Steventon. He married twice : (1) in 1792, Anne Mathew, daughter of General and Lady Jane Mathew, of Laverstoke Manor House, near Overton, who died in 1795 : (2) in 1797, Mary Lloyd. By his second wife, James was father of James Edward Austen-Leigh, author of the *Memoir*, and of his sister Caroline. By the first, he was father of one daughter, Anne, *b.* April, 1793, who married Ben Lefroy (*q.v.*). James Austen died in 1819.

Austen, Jane, the novelist, *b.* December 16, 1775, at Steventon Parsonage, Hants. She was the seventh child of George and Cassandra Austen. When very young she and her sister C. lived for a short time at Oxford and Southampton, under the care of Mrs. Cawley, a sister of Dr. Cooper (*q.v.*). Afterwards they were both at Mrs. Latournelle's school at Reading, and came home in 1784 or 1785. The sisters and their mother visited Bath in 1797, and J. was there again, with her brother Edward and his wife in 1799. The Austen family moved to Bath in 1801 (*see* **Austen, George** (1)), and in the following year J. visited Dawlish and Teignmouth. At one or the other of these places occurred her " one real romance," sadly ended by the premature death of her presumed lover. (*See Life*, 89, 90.) The Austens were at Lyme Regis in September, 1804. After the death of the father in January, 1805, Mrs. Austen and the two sisters visited

Clifton, Adlestrop Rectory, and Stoneleigh Abbey. They then went to Southampton (*q.v.*), living first in lodgings, and from March, 1807, in Castle Square. In 1809 they moved to Chawton (*q.v.*), where most of Jane's work was done. " Between February, 1811, and August, 1816, she began and completed *Mansfield Park*, *Emma*, and *Persuasion* " (*Mem.*, vi.). Her health began to fail in 1816, and she became seriously ill in March–April, 1817. In May, 1817, " she was persuaded to remove to Winchester, for the sake of medical advice from Mr. Lyford " (*Mem.* xi.) Jane and her sister lodged in College Street, where she died on July 18, 1817. On the 24th she was buried in Winchester Cathedral, near the " centre of the north aisle, almost opposite to the beautiful chantry tomb of William of Wykeham " (*Mem.* xi).

For the dates of composition and publication of Jane Austen's works, *see* their various titles.

Austen, Philadelphia, sister of Jane's father. She married T. S. Hancock—*See* **Hancock.**

Austen-Leigh, James Edward, *b.* November 17, 1798, the author of the *Memoir*. He was the son of Jane's eldest brother, James, by his second wife. He died in 1874. Cf. **Lloyd, Mary.**

Avignon, where Colonel Brandon's sister was ill. *S.S.* xiii.

Aylmers, The. Mrs. R. has been spending the Easter with the Aylmers at Twickenham. *M.P.*xlv.

B

Baddeley, Sir Thomas Bertram's butler. *M.P.*xix.

Bahama. We do not call Bermuda or Bahama, you know, the West Indies. *Pers.* viii.

Baker Street, *See* **London.**

Baldwin, Admiral. A certain Admiral Baldwin, the most deplorable-looking person you can imagine ; his face the colour of mahogany, rough and rugged to the last degree, all lines and wrinkles, nine gray hairs of a side, and nothing but a dab of powder at top. *Pers.* iii.

Baly-craig, the country seat of the Dixons, near Dublin. *E.*xix.

Banbury. I may perhaps get as far as Banbury to-day. *M.P.*xx.

Bank, The. *See* **London.**

Barnet. After making every possible inquiry. . . at the inns in Barnet and Hatfield. *P.P.*xlvi.

" Baronetage The," the only book Sir Walter Elliot ever took up. *Pers.* i.

Bartlett's Buildings, Holborn. *See* **London.**

Barton, a village four miles north of Exeter. *S.S.*iv. The village of Barton was chiefly on one of these hills, and formed a pleasant view from the cottage windows. *S.S.*vi.

Barton Cottage, where Elinor and Marianna Dashwood

and their mother lived. *S.S*.iv. As a house Barton Cottage, though small, was comfortable and compact. *S.S*.vi.

Barton Cross. We will walk to Sir John's new plantations at Barton Cross. *S.S*.xlvi.

Barton Park, Sir John Middleton's seat. *S.S*.iv. The house was large and handsome. *S.S*.vii.

Barton Valley—a pleasant fertile spot, well wooded and rich in pasture. *S.S*.vi.

Basingstoke, Hants., where the monthly assemblies provided many dancing occasions for Jane and Cassandra.

Bates, Mrs., widow of a former vicar of Highbury. *E*.ii. A " quiet, neat old lady." *E*.xix.

Bates, Hetty, her daughter. *E*.ii. [Her] active, talking daughter, almost ready to overpower them with care and kindness, thanks for their visit, solicitude for their shoes, anxious inquiries after Mr. Woodhouse's health, cheerful communications about her mother's, and sweet-cake from the buffet. *E*.xix.

Bates, Jane. *See* **Fairfax.**

Bath. (1) J.A. with her sister Cassandra and their mother, visited Bath in 1797, and J. was again there with her brother Edward and his wife in 1799. " The family removed to Bath in the spring of 1801, where they resided first at No. 4 Sydney Terrace [should be Sydney Place] and afterwards in Green Park Buildings." (*Mem.* iv.) After the father's death, the daughters and their mother lodged for a short time at No. 25,

Gay Street. (2) I had allowed her . . . to go to Bath with one of her young friends. *S.S.*xxxi. (3) Dear Mary, I am just arrived. Bath seems full, and everything as usual, yours sincerely. *M.P.*vi. (4) He is going for his health to Bath, where if the waters are favourable to his constitution and my wishes, he will be laid up with the gout many weeks. *Lady S.* Lett. 26. (5) Symptoms of the Gout and a Winter at Bath. *Sand.* ii. (6) Beware of the unmeaning Luxuries of Bath. *L. & F.* 7. (7) "Les. C." in *L & F.* 49. (8) " Scraps " in *L. & F.* 131.

Bath : Localities :—

1. **Argyle Buildings.** *N.A.*xi.

2. **Bath Street.** (1) The last time we met was in Bath Street. *N.A.*xxvii. (2) Mrs. Charles Musgrove saw Mr. Walter Elliot and Miss Clay " turn the corner from Bath Street." *Pers.* xxii.

3. **Beacon Hill.** *Life,* 129.

4. **Beechen Cliff.** Beechen Cliff, that noble hill, whose beautiful verdure and hanging coppice render it so striking an object from almost every opening in Bath. *N.A.*xiv.

5. **Belmont.** The Admiral had made up his mind not to begin till they had gained the greater space and quiet of Belmont. *Pers.* xviii.

6. **Bond Street.** (1) Catherine. . . walked out into the town, and in Bond Street overtook the second Miss Thorpe. *N.A.*xiv. (2) The worst of Bath was, the number of its plain women . . . once, he had stood

in a shop in Bond Street, he had counted eighty-seven women go by . . . without there being a tolerable face among them. *Pers.* xv.

7. **Broad Street.** *N.A.*xi.

8. **Brook Street.** They were turning the corner into Brook Street, when he had overtaken them. *N.A.* xiii.

9. **Camden Place,** where Sir Walter Elliot took a house. *Pers.* xiii.

10. **Cheap Street.** Everybody acquainted with Bath may remember the difficulties of crossing Cheap Street at this point [the archway, opposite Union Passage]. *N.A.*vii.

11. **Claverton Down.** Did not we agree together to take a drive this morning? . . . We are going up Claverton Down. *N.A.*ix. There was "a favourite duelling ground on Claverton Down" (Meehan *Famous Houses of Bath*, etc., 1901, 25).

12. **Crescent, The.** (1) *Life*, 130. (2) They hastened away to the Crescent, to breathe the fresh air of better company. *N.A.*v.

13. **Edgar's Buildings.** What say you to going to Edgar's Buildings with me, and looking at my new hat? *N.A.*vi. The Thorpes lodged in Edgar's Buildings.

14. **Gay Street.** (1) No. 25, the lodgings to which Mrs. Austen and her daughters moved after the father's death, 1805. *Life*, 183. (2) Admiral and Mrs. Croft lodged in Gay Street. *Pers.* xviii.

15. **Green Park Buildings**, No. 27, to which the Austen family moved about the beginning of 1805. *Life*, 172.

16. **Hermitage Walk.** Instead of waiting for me, you took the volume into the Hermitage Walk, and I was obliged to stay till you had finished it. *N.A*.xiv.

17. **Lansdown Crescent.** They knew he was to dine in Lansdown Crescent. *Pers.* xv.

18. **Lansdown Hill.** I will drive you up Lansdown Hill to-morrow. *N.A*.vii.

19. **Lansdown Road.** I saw him at that moment turn up the Lansdown Road, driving a smart-looking girl. *N.A*.xi.

20. **Laura Place.** (1) They passed briskly down Pulteney Street and through Laura Place. *N.A*.xi. (2) Lady Dalrymple took a house in Laura Place. *Pers.* xvi.

21. **Lower Rooms.** They made their appearance in the Lower Rooms ; and here fortune was more favourable to our heroine. *N.A*.iii. The Lower Assembly Rooms were burned down in 1820.

22. **Market Place.** In another moment she was herself whisked into the Market Place. *N.A*.xi.

23. **Marlborough Buildings.** Colonel Wallis . . . was living in very good style in Marlborough Buildings. *Pers.* xv.

24. **Milsom Street.** (1) I saw the prettiest hat you can imagine in a shop-window in Milsom Street. *N.A*.vi. (2) In walking up Milsom Street, she had

the good fortune to meet with the Admiral. *Pers.*
xviii. " Milsom Street is now the great thorough-
fare from everywhere to everywhere, and every one
goes to if for everything. It is the Regent Street
of Bath, and, like Regent Street, is on an incline."
(Meehan. *Famous Houses of Bath*, etc., 1901, 193.)

25. **Molland's.** She, Anne, and Mrs. Clay, therefore,
turned into Molland's. *Pers.* xix. A Bath con-
fectioner's shop.

26. **Old Bridge.** Driving through the long course of
streets from the Old Bridge to Camden Place.
Pers. xiv.

27. **Paragon Buildings,** where the Leigh Perrots
lodged in 1799. *Life*, 127.

28. **Pulteney Street.** (1) They [Catherine Morland
and the Allens], were soon settled in comfortable
lodgings in Pulteney Street. *N.A.*ii. (2) In return-
ing down Pulteney Street, she distinguished him
on the right-hand pavement. *Pers.* xix.

29. **Pump Room.** (1) Every morning now brought
its regular duties . . . the Pump Room to be attended.
*N.A.*iii. (2) Mary, well amused as she generally
was in her station at a window overlooking the
entrance to the Pump Room. *Pers.* xxii.

30. **Pump Yard.** (1) Half a minute conducted them
through the Pump-yard to the archway, opposite
Union Passage. *N.A.*vii. (2) I met with Mr.
Elliot in Bath Street . . . . He turned back and
walked with me to the Pump Yard. *Pers.* xxii.

31. **Queen Square.** (1) We must be in a good situation

—none of your Queen Squares for us! *Pers.* vi. (2) No. 13 was where the Austens (including J.A.) lodged in 1799. *Life,* 127.

32. **Rivers Street.** Lady Russell then drove to her own lodgings in Rivers Street. *Pers.* xiv.

33. **Sion Hill.** *Life,* 168.

34. **Sydney Gardens.** There is a public breakfast in Sydney Gardens every morning, so that we shall not be wholly starved. *Life,* 129. The Gardens were also the scene of concerts, illuminations, and fireworks. *Life,* 130, 131. These Gardens were laid out in 1775.

35. **Sydney Terrace (Place),** No. 4, where the Austen family settled in 1801. *Life,* 172.

36. **Union Passage.** The archway, opposite Union Passage. *N.A.*vii.

37. **Union Street.** Mr. Elliot (always obliging) just setting off for Union Street on a commission of Mrs. Clay's. *Pers.* xix.

38. **Upper Rooms.** (1) J.A. mentions dancing in them. *Life,* 167. (2) The important evening came which was to usher her into the Upper Rooms. *N.A.*ii. The Upper Rooms were opened in 1771.

39. **Westgate Buildings,** where Mrs. Smith lodged. *Pers.* xvii. " Westgate Buildings must have been rather surprised by the appearance of a carriage drawn up near its pavement !" observed Sir Walter. *Ibid.* xvii.

Although Sir Walter Elliot sneered at them, Westgate Buildings contained the famous Hetling House, where George II's daughter, Princess Mary, was entertained in 1740. "In fact it was the only building, with the exception of the Royal Apartments in the immediate neighbourhood (on the West Gate) sufficiently extensive or important to meet the requirements of royalty." (Meehan, *Famous Houses of Bath*, etc., 1901, 5.)

40. **White Hart Inn.** (1) A trunk, directed to *The Rev. Philip Elton, White Hart Inn, Bath.* E.xxiii. (2) They were come to Bath for a few days . . . and were at the White Hart. *Pers.* xxii. The White Hart stood in Stall Street. It was closed in 1864 and demolished in 1867. On the site of this and other buildings now stands the Grand Pump-Room Hotel. (Peach, *Historic Houses in Bath*, 1883, 20.)

41. **Wick Rocks.** I heard Tilney hallooing . . . that they were going as far as Wick Rocks. *N.A.* xi. "The most remarkable natural objects in the parish [of Wick] are perhaps the Wick Rocks, which line each side of a deep glen, about a mile in extent, and rise in varying height right and left of the valley. (Meehan. *More Famous Houses of Bath*, 1906, 90.)

Bath Street. *See* **Bath.**

Battel [Battle], Sussex. On the other side of Battel— quite down in the Weald. *Sand.* i.

Bayle, Mr., carpenter at Steventon. *Life*, 142.

Beachy Head. Brighton is almost by Beachy Head. *M.P.* xxv.

Beacon Hill. *See* **Bath.**

Beard, Mr., Solicitor, Gray's Inn : a visitor at Sanditon. *Sand.* vi.

Beaufort, Miss, and **Letitia Beaufort.** Just such young ladies as may be met with, in at least one family out of three, throughout the kingdom. *Sand.* xi.

Beaulieu Abbey. " H. of E." in *L. & F.* 88.

Bedford, The. *See* **London.**

Bedfordshire. *L. & F.* 10.

Bedford Square. *See* **London.**

Beechen Cliff. *See* **Bath.**

"Beggar's Petition, The," [by Rev. T. Moss, *q.v.*]. *N.A.*i.

"Belinda," [by Miss Edgeworth, 1801]. *N.A.*v.

Belle—" my dear Belle." " C. of L." in *L. & F.* 105.

Bellevue Cottage, Sanditon. *Sand.* iv.

Belmont. *See* **Bath.**

Bennet, Mr. Mr. Bennet was so odd a mixture of quick parts, sarcastic humour, reserve, and caprice, that the experience of three-and-twenty years had been insufficient to make his wife understand his character. *P.P.*i.

Bennet, Mrs., *née* Gardiner, daughter of an attorney at Meryton. She was a woman of mean understanding, little information, and uncertain temper. When she was discontented, she fancied herself nervous. The business of her life was to get her daughters married : its solace was visiting and news. *P.P.*i.

Bennet, Catharine (Kitty) and **Lydia.** *P.P.*ii. The two youngest of the family, Catherine and Lydia . . . their minds were more vacant than their sisters. *P.P.*vii.

Bennet, Elizabeth, second daughter of the Bennets, and the heroine of the story. *P.P.*i, ii. Elizabeth . . . had a lively, playful disposition, which delighted in anything ridiculous. *P.P.*iii.

Bennet, Jane, eldest daughter of the Bennets. *P.P.*i. " You were dancing with the only handsome girl in the room," said Mr. Darcy, looking at the eldest Miss Bennet. *P.P.*iii.

Bennet, Mary. " What say you, Mary ? for you are a young lady of deep reflection, I know, and read great books, and make extracts." Mary wished to say something very sensible, but knew not how. *P.P.*ii.

Benwick, Captain James, friend of Capt. Harville. *Pers.* xi. He had been engaged to Fanny Harville, who died ; later engaged to Louisa Musgrove. The dejected, thinking, feeling, reading Captain Benwick. *Pers.* xviii.

Beresford, Colonel. I am going to dance these two dances with Colonel Beresford. *Watsons,* 319.

Berkeley Street. *See* **London.**

Berkshire. " Les. C." in *L. & F.* 58.

Bermuda. *Pers.* viii. (*See* **Bahama.**)

Bernard, Mr. Mr. Bernard . . . recollected that his Servant had got his white Gloves, and immediately ran out to fetch them. " C. of L." in *L. & F.* iii.

Bertha. *See* **St. Clair.**

Bertram, Sir Thomas, Bart., M.P., of Mansfield Park, in the county of Northampton. *M.P.*i.

Bertram, Lady, *née* Maria Ward, of Huntingdon. A woman of very languid feelings, and a temper remarkably easy and indolent. *M.P.*i.

Bertram, Edmund, younger son of the Bertrams. The character of Edmund, his strong good sense, and uprightness of mind, bid most fairly for utility, honour and happiness to himself and all his connexions. *M.P.*i, ii.

Bertram, Julia, younger daughter. I hope she will not tease my poor pug . . . I have but just got Julia to leave it alone. *M.P.*i, ii.

Bertram, Maria, elder daughter. *M.P.*ii.

Bertram, Tom, elder son. His eldest son was careless and extravagant, and had already given him much uneasiness. *M.P.*i, ii.

Betty, Mrs. Jennings's maid. It will only be sending Betty by the coach, and I hope I can afford *that*. *S.S.*xxv.

Bickerton, Miss, a parlour boarder at Mrs. Goddard's. *E*.xxxix.

Bigg, Alethea, a daughter of Mr. Bigg Wither of Manydown, to whom J.A. wrote on January 24, 1817. (*Mem.* xi.) She was a close friend of J.A. Cf. **Heathcote.**

Bigg, Catherine, sister of Alethea : she *m.* the Rev. Herbert Hill, Southey's uncle.

Bingley, Caroline, sister of Charles. His sisters were fine women, with an air of decided fashion. *P.P.*iii.

Bingley, Charles. *P.P.*i. He was quite young, wonderfully handsome, extremely agreeable, and, to crown the whole, he meant to be at the next assembly with a large party. *P.P.*iii.

Bingley, Louisa. *See* **Hurst.**

Bird, Mrs., *née* Milman. *E*.xxxii.

Birmingham. (1) *P.P.*xlii. (2) They came from Birmingham, which is not a place to promise much, you know, Mr. Weston. *E*.xxxvi.

Blackall, Mr. Fellow of Emmanuel College, Cambridge, an early admirer of J.A. (*Life*, 85, 86.)

Blair [Hugh], The author of *Lectures on Rhetoric*, etc., (1) *N.A.*xiv. (2) His *Sermons*. Supposing the preacher. to have the sense to prefer Blair's to his own. *M.P.*ix.

Blaize Castle, near Kingsweston Down, Bath. The finest place in England . . . worth going fifty miles at any time to see. *N.A.*xi.

Blake, Mrs., a widow, sister of Mr. Howard. *Watsons*, 317.

Blake, Charles, her son, ten years old. *Ibid.*, 318.

Blenheim, Oxon. *P.P.*xlii.

Bond, John, Mr. Austen's " factotum " in farming operations at Steventon. *Lett.* i, 151, 161, 174, 249.

Bond Street, Bath. *See* **Bath.**

Bond Street, London. *See* **London.**

Bonomi, an architect. My friend Lord Courtland . . .

laid before me three different plans of Bonomi's. *S.S.*xxxvi. This was Joseph Bonomi, A.R.A., 1739–1808.

Bookham, Surrey, where the Cookes (*q.v.*) lived. It was visited by Mrs. Austen and her daughters on their leaving Southampton in 1809, and by J.A. in 1814. *Life,* 304. It is possible that while at Bookham, J.A. may have met Madame d'Arblay (Fanny Burney), whose books she knew well. Cf. **Little Bookham.**

Bosworth, Battle of. " H. of E." in *L. & F.* 87.

Bowen, Mr., the doctor who attended Mrs. Austen at Bath. *Life,* 173.

Box Hill. Emma had never been to Box Hill ; she wished to see what everybody found so well worth seeing. *E.*xlii.

Brabourne, Lord. *See* **Knight, Fanny Catherine.**

Bragge, Mr. Twice in one week he and Mr. Bragge went to London and back again with four horses. *E.*xxxvi.

Bragge, Mrs., a cousin of Mr. Suckling. *E.*xxv.

Braithwaite family, The. *E.*xiv.

Bramston, Mr. and Mrs., of Oakley Hall, visited by J.A. *Life,* 142.

Brand, Admiral, who once played a shabby trick on Admiral Croft. *Pers.* xviii.

Brandon, Colonel, a friend of Sir John Middleton, a bachelor " on the wrong side of five-and-thirty." *S.S.*vii.

Brandon, Eliza, ward and niece of Col. Brandon's father, *m.* his brother. *S.S.*xxxi.

Brereton, Miss, *m.* (1) Mr. Hollis, (2) Sir Harry Denham. *See* **Denham, Lady.**

Brereton, Clara, companion to Lady Denham. *Sand.* iii, vi.

" Bride of Abydos, The " [by Byron]. *Pers.* xi.

Bridges, Sir Brook, of Goodnestone, Kent. His daughter Elizabeth married Edward Austen (*q.v.*), 1791.

Bridges, Edward, who made himself pleasant to J. when she was visiting at Goodnestone Farm, 1805. *Life,* 191.

Bridget. She was very plain and her name was Bridget. . . . Nothing therefore could be expected from her. *L. & F.* 32.

Brigden, Captain, a friend of Admiral Croft. Brigden stares to see anybody with me but my wife. *Pers.* xviii.

Brighthelmstone. " Les. C." in *L. & F.* 58.

Brighton. (1). *P.P.*xxxix. (2) Brighton is almost as gay in winter as in summer. *M.P.*xxi. (3) Your large, overcrowded places, like Brighton . . . *Sand.* i.

Brinshore—that paltry Hamlet. *Sand.* i.

Bristol, (1) whence came Mrs. Elton. *E.*xxii. (2) *S.S.*xxxix. (3) *N.A.*xi. (4) " Les. C." in *L. & F.* 52.

British Gallery. *See* **London.**

Broadway Lane, Highbury. Miss Taylor and I met with him [Mr. Weston] in Broadway Lane, when, because

C

it began to mizzle, he darted away . . . and borrowed two umbrellas for us. *E*.i.

Brockham. where General Tilney's surveyor lived. *N.A*.xxvi.

Bromley, Kent, where horses were changed on the journey from Hunsford to Longbourn. *P.P*.xxxvii.

Bromley, Mrs., the landlady of the house in Queen Square, Bath, where the Austens stayed in 1799. *Life,* 128.

Brompton. *See* **London.**

Brook Street. *See* **Bath.**

Brown, Dr. and Mrs., visitors at Sanditon. *Sand*. vi.

Brown, Mary. Publishing the banns of marriage between John Smith and Mary Brown. *S.S*.xli.

Brown, Mrs. Mrs. Brown, and the other women at the Commissioner's, at Gibraltar. *M.P*.xxiv.

Brown, Mrs. The party at Mrs. Brown's. *E*.xxii.

Browne, Isaac Hawkins—his " Address to Tobacco." *M.P*.xvii.

Brunswick Square. *See* **London.**

Buckingham, in " **Henry VIII.**" *M.P.* xxxiv.

Buckingham, Duke of, George Villiers. "H. of E." in *L. & F.* 95.

Bullen, Anna. *Ibid.* 89.

Burgess, Mrs. I was very glad to give her five guineas to take her down to Exeter, where she thinks of staying three or four weeks with Mrs. Burgess. *S.S*.xlix.

Burleigh, Lord. " H. of E." in *L. & F.* 91.

Burney, Fanny : her *Camilla, N.A.*v. and *Cecilia' N.A.*v.

Burns, Robert. If ever there was a man who *felt*, it was Burns. *Sand.* vii.

Burton-on-Trent. *Ibid.* xii.

Butler, The rhyming, a character in *Lovers' Vows* (*q.v.*). *M.P.*xiv.

Byron, Lord. Talking as before of Mr. Scott and Lord Byron. *Pers.* xii. *See* also **Bride of Abydos** and **Giaour.**

C

Cadell, Mr., the London publisher to whom *Pride and Prejudice* was offered in 1797 by J.A.'s father, and who declined it by return of post.

Camberwell. *See* **London.**

Cambridge. My plan was laid at Westminster [School], a little altered, perhaps, at Cambridge, and at one-and-twenty executed. *M.P.*vi.

Camden Place. *See* **Bath.**

" Camilla," by Fanny Burney. (1) J.'s name appeared in the list of subscribers, 1796. (2) It is only *Cecilia*, or *Camilla*, or *Belinda*. *N.A.*v. (3) She took up a Book ; it happened to be a vol. of *Camilla. Sand.* vi.

Campbell, the poet.   Campbell in his pleasures of Hope has touched the extreme of our Sensations.   *Sand.* vii.

Campbell, Colonel, a friend of Jane Fairfax's father. *E*.xii.

Campbell, Mrs.   I suppose Colonel and Mrs. Campbell will not be able to part with her [Jane Fairfax] at all. *E*.xii.

Campbell, Mr., surgeon of the *Thrush.*   *M.P.*xxxviii.

" Canopus," The, a ship at Portsmouth.   *M.P.*xxxviii.

Canterbury, visited by J.A. in 1813.   *Life,* 285.

Cape, The [of Good Hope].   This was drawn at the Cape.   He met with a clever young German artist at the Cape.   *Pers.* xxiii.

Capper, Miss.   You must have heard me mention Miss Capper.   *Sand.* ix.

Car [*sic*], James I's favourite.   " H. of E." in *L. & F.* 95.

Caractacus.   *N.A.*xiv.

Careys, The Miss.   Here are the two Miss Careys come over from Newton.   *S.S.*xiii.

Carlton House.   *See* **London.**

Carmarthen.   " Scraps " in *L. & F.* 138.

Carr, Miss Fanny, a friend of Miss Osborne.   *Watsons,* 317.

Carter, Captain, one of the officers at Meryton.   Lydia ... continued to express her admiration of Captain Carter. *P.P.*vii.

Carteret, The Hon. Miss, daughter of the Dowager Viscountess Dalrymple. *Pers.* xvi, xix.

Cartwright, perhaps Mrs. Jennings's housekeeper. *S.S.* xxvi.

Cassel, Count, a character in *Lovers' Vows* (*q.v.*), *M.P.*xiii.

" Castle of Wolfenbach." *N.A.*vi. This was by Mrs. Parsons, and was published in 1793.

Catherine of France. " H. of E." in *L. & F.* 85.

Cawley, Mrs., a sister of Dr. Cooper (*q.v.*) When very young Jane and her sister Cassandra were for a short time under her care at Oxford and Southampton.

" Cecilia." *N.A.*v. By Fanny Burney. *See* **Camilla.**

Cecilia. Robertus . . . with his Lady the amiable Cecilia. " Scraps " in *L. & F.* 140.

Chamberlayne, an officer at Meryton. *P.P.*xxxix.

Chamberlayne, Mrs., a Bath acquaintance. *Life,* 165, 168, etc.

Chapman, Mrs., Lady Bertram's own maid. *M.P.*xxvii.

Charlecombe, a village near Bath, " which is sweetly situated in a little green valley, as a village with such a name ought to be." *Life,* 129.

Charles, a character in " The First Act of a Comedy." " Scraps " in *L. & F.* 133.

Charles, a groom at Mansfield Park. *M.P.*xx.

Charles—, Sir, a friend of Admiral Crawford. Sir

Charles was much delighted in having such an opportunity of proving his regard for Admiral Crawford. *M.P.*xxxi.

Charles I. " H. of E." in *L. & F.* 95.

Charmouth, near Lyme Regis. Charmouth, with its high grounds and extensive sweeps of country, and still more its sweet retired bay, backed by dark cliffs. . . . *Pers.* xi.

Chatsworth. The celebrated beauties of Matlock, Chatsworth, Dovedale, or the Peak. *P.P.*xlii.

Chawton Cottage. In 1809 Jane Austen's brother Edward offered his mother and sisters Chawton Cottage as a residence, and they settled there, with Miss Lloyd, a near connexion, in that year. (*Mem.* iv.) Jane lived there till she went to Winchester to die. Chawton village is about a mile from Alton, Hants. " Chawton must also be considered the place most closely connected with her career as a writer ; for there it was that, in the maturity of her mind, she either wrote, or re-arranged, and prepared for publication the books by which she has become known to the world." (*Mem.* iv.)

Chawton House, Hants., a residence of Thomas Knight (*q.v.*) later the property of Edward Austen, Jane's brother, who took the name of Knight. *See* **Austen, Edward.**

Cheapside. *See* **London.**

Cheap Street. *See* **Bath.**

Cheltenham. (1) J.A. and her sister spent three weeks

there in 1816. *Life*, 334. (2) I do not call Tunbridge or Cheltenham the country. *M.P.*xxi.

Cheshire, the county in which the Elliot family had first been settled. *Pers.* i.

Chichester. (1) *Sand.* ix. (2) She has been trying to make some match at Chichester—she won't tell us with whom. *Watsons*, 301.

" Children of the Abbey," which Robert Martin had never read. *E.*iv. This was by Regina Maria Roche, and was published in 1798.

China. *M.P.*xvi.

Chloe, a character in " The First Act of a Comedy." " Scraps " in *L. & F.* 133.

Cholmeley, Jane. *See* **Perrot.**

Christ Church [Oxford]. It was built for a Christ Church man, a friend of mine, a very good sort of fellow. *N.A.*vii.

Churchill, the home of the Vernons, in Sussex. *Lady S.* Lett. i.

Churchill, Frank [Weston], son of Mr. Weston, adopted by Mr. and Mrs. Churchill, of Enscombe. He took the name of Churchill on coming of age. *E.*ii. He was a *very* good-looking young man ; height, air, address, all were unexceptionable, and his countenance had a good deal of the spirit and liveliness of his father's ; he looked quick and sensible. *E.*xxiii.

Churchill, Miss, sister of Mr. Churchill, first wife of Mr.

Weston, and mother of Frank. She wanted at once to be the wife of Captain Weston, and Miss Churchill of Enscombe. *E*.ii.

Churchill, Mr., of Enscombe, Yorkshire. *E*.ii. Mr. Churchill has pride ; but his pride is nothing to his wife's. *E*.xxxvi.

Churchill, Mrs., his wife. *E*.ii. Mrs. Churchill, after being disliked at least twenty-five years, was now [when dead] spoken of with compassionate allowances. *E*.xlv.

Clapham, Surrey. (1) He did trace them easily to Clapham, but no farther. *P.P.*xlvi. (2) *Sand.* ix.

Clara. " Scraps " in *L. & F.* 138.

Clarke, The Rev. James Stanier, who, instructed by the Prince Regent, showed J.A. the library and other apartments at Carlton House, and also made some rather absurd suggestions as to novels J. should write. After serving as a naval chaplain he became domestic chaplain and librarian to the Prince of Wales (later Prince Regent) in 1799.

Clarke, Louisa, Louisa Clarke (said I) is in general a very pleasant Girl, yet sometimes her good humour is clouded by Peevishness, Envy and Spite. " Scraps " in *L. & F.* 132.

Clarke, Mrs. An intimate acquaintance of Mrs. Jennings. *S.S.*xxxviii.

Clarke's Library, Meryton. *P.P.*vii.

Clarkes, The, in Staffordshire. *Lady S.,* Lett. 16.

Claudia, Laura's mother. *L. & F.* 10. Cf. **St. Clair.**

Claverton Down. *See* **Bath.**

Clay, Mrs. Penelope, daughter of Mr. Shepherd, Sir Walter Elliot's agent, and friend of Elizabeth Elliot : in the end the mistress of Mr. W. W. Elliot. *Pers.* ii, iii.

Clayton Park, near Highbury. *E.*viii.

"Cleopatra," The, a ship at Portsmouth. *M.P.*xxxviii.

" Clermont," a novel, *N.A.*vi. This was by Regina Maria Roche, and was published in 1798.

Clermont, Lord and Lady. " C. of L." in *L. & F.* 113.

Cleveland, the home of the Palmers. *S.S.*xx. A spacious, modern-built house, situated on a sloping lawn. *S.S.*xlii.

Cleveland, Mr., brother of Mrs. Marlowe. " Les. C." in *L. & F.* 59.

Clifton, near Bristol, (1) was visited by J. with her sister and mother, after their Bath home was broken up in 1805. (2) If she is really ill, why not go to Bath . . . or to Clifton ? *E.*xxxvi. (3) We shall drive directly to Clifton, and dine there. *N.A.*xi.

Clifton, York Hotel. They had driven directly to the York Hotel, ate some soup, and bespoke an early dinner. *N.A.*xv.

Coachman, Mrs. Sheldon's, who " sprained his foot as he was cleaning the Carriage." *Sand.* v.

Cobb, The, Lyme Regis. *Pers.* xi. Louisa Musgrove fell from it. *Ibid.* xii.

Cobham, Surrey, (1) where J. and her brother Henry spent a night on their journey up to London in March, 1814. (*Life*, 291). (2) There was no scarlet fever at Cobham. *E*.xi.

Cobham, Lord. " H. of E." in *L. & F.* 85.

Cole, Mr. *E*.ix, xxvi.

Cole, Mrs., *E*.xix, xxvi. The Coles had been settled some years in Highbury, and were very good sort of people, friendly, liberal, and unpretending ; but, on the other hand, they were of low origin, in trade, and only moderately genteel. *E*.xxv.

" Collection of Letters, A," with an alliterative dedication to Miss Cooper, printed for the first time, with other Juvenilia, in *Love and Freindship*, 1922, pp. 99–126.

Columella. *S.S.*xix. The reference is to Vol. II. ch. xxviii of Richard Graves's *Columella ; or the Distressed Anchoret*, 1779. See *Notes and Queries* for November 28, 1914.

Combe, Willoughby's home. *S.S.*xiv. **Combe Magna** xvii.

Commissioner, The, at Gibraltar. *M.P.*xxiv.

Compton, the home of Rushworth's friend Smith. I wish you could see Compton . . . it is the most complete thing . . . The approach *now* is one of the finest things in the country ; you see the house in the most surprising manner. *M.P.*vi.

Conduit Street. *See* **London.**

Cook at South End, The. . . . never had been able to understand what she meant by a basin of nice smooth gruel, thin, but not too thin. *E*.xii.

Cooke, The Rev. George Leigh, cousin of J. A. (*See* **Leigh, Cassandra** (1)). Tutor at Corpus Christi College, Oxford—*See Mem.* iv. J.A. says (1805)—"my cousin George was very kind, and talked sense to me every now and then." *Life*, 186.

Cooke, Samuel. *See* **Leigh, Cassandra** (1).

Cooper, Dr. Edward and Mrs. He was rector of Whaddon near Bath, and later, vicar of Sonning, Berkshire. He *m.* Jane Leigh, Mrs. Austen's eldest sister. She died in 1783. Dr. Cooper had also a house at Southcote, near Reading. He died in 1792.

Cooper, Edward and Jane, cousins of J.A., were the children of Dr. and Mrs. Cooper. "After the death of their own parents, the two young Coopers paid long visits at Steventon." (*Mem.* ii.) To Jane, J.A. dedicated the "Collection of Letters" printed in *Love and Freindship* (p. 101). Edward at Oxford gained the prize for Latin hexameters on *Hortus Anglicus* in 1791 ; later he wrote several volumes of sermons. He became rector of Hamstall-Ridware, Staffordshire, in 1799. Jane *m.* Captain, afterwards Sir Thomas Williams "under whom Charles Austen served in several ships." A few years after her marriage she was killed suddenly in a carriage accident. (August 1798.)

Cooper, Mrs. James, *née* Milman. *E*.xxxiii.

Cope, Mrs. " C. of L." in *L. & F.* 103.

Cork, Ireland. *Pers.* viii.

Cork Street. *See* **London.**

Cornwall. Ecclesford, the seat of the Right Hon. Lord Ravenshaw, in Cornwall. *M.P.*xiii.

Corydon. *The Mystery* in *Mem.* iii.

Cottager and **Cottager's wife,** characters in *Lovers' Vows* (*q.v.*). *M.P.*xiv.

Courteney, General. The Marquis of Longtown and General Courteney . . . some of my very old friends. *N.A.*xvii.

Courtland, Lord. *S.S.*xxxvi.

Covent Garden Theatre. *See* **London.**

Cowper, the poet. (1) Nay, mamma, if he is not to be animated by Cowper !—but we must allow for difference of taste. *S.S.*iii. (2) Fanny Price quotes from *The Task,* I. " The Sofa," l. 338. *M.P.*vi. (3) Fanny Price thinks of *Tirocinium,* l. 562. *M.P.* xlv. (4) Like Cowper and his fire at twilight— " Myself creating what I saw " [*Task,* IV, l. 290]. *E.*xli. (5) *Sand.* i.

Cox, Anne, sister of William. *E.*xxvii.

Cox, William. A pert young lawyer. *E.*xvi.

Cox. Another Miss Cox, unnamed, and a second young Cox. *E.*xxix.

Crabbe's " Tales." Here are Crabbe's *Tales,* and the *Idler,* at hand to relieve you, if you tire of your great book. *M.P.*xvi. The allusion is to the *Tales* published in 1812.

Craven, Lord, who took his kinsman, Thomas Fowle
(C.'s fiancé) to the West Indies, as chaplain to his
regiment, where Fowle died of yellow fever.   Craven
" said afterwards that, had he known of his engagement, he would not have allowed him to go to so
dangerous a climate." *Life*, 105.

Crawford, Admiral and Mrs., of Hill Street, London ;
uncle and aunt of Henry and Mary Crawford.   Admiral and Mrs. Crawford, though agreeing in nothing
else, were united in affection for these children.
*M.P.*iv.

Crawford, Henry, half-brother of Mrs. Grant.   Henry,
though not handsome, had air and countenance.
*M.P.*iv.

Crawford, Mary, Henry's sister.   Mary Crawford was
remarkably pretty.   *M.P.*iv.

Crawfords, The.   I am not conscious of being more
sincerely attached to Willoughby than I was to Neville,
Fitzowen, or either of the Crawfords, for all of whom
I once felt the most lasting affection that ever warmed
a Woman's heart.   " C. of L." in *L. & F.* 105.

Crescent, The.   *See* **Bath.**

Crewkerne.   Going on now for Crewkerne, in his way
to Bath and London.   *Pers.* xii.

" Critic," Sheridan's.   " H. of E." in *L. & F.* 95.

Croft, Admiral, tenant of Kellynch Hall.   Admiral
Croft was a very hale, hearty, well-looking man,

a little weather-beaten, to be sure, but not much, and quite the gentleman in all his notions and behaviour. *Pers.* iii, v.

Croft, Sophia, *née* Wentworth, his wife. A very well-spoken genteel, shrewd lady, she seemed to be. *Pers.* iii, v.

Cromer. Perry was a week at Cromer once, and he holds it to be the best of all the sea-bathing places. *E*.xii.

Cromwell, in *Henry VIII. M.P*.xxxiv.

Cromwell [Oliver]. " H. of C." in *L. & F.* 96.

Crosby & Son, Messrs., of London, to whom the MS. of *Northanger Abbey*, under the title of *Susan*, was sold for £10 in 1803. (*Life*, 174.) It was not published by them, but was bought back for £10 by one of J.'s brothers, probably Henry, about 1815.

Crown Inn. The, Highbury. He had business at the Crown about his hay. *E*.xxiii.

Crown Inn, The, Portsmouth. He had reached it [Portsmouth] late the night before . . . was staying at the Crown. *M.P*.xli.

Croydon. He will no more follow her to Croydon now than he did last March. *Watsons*, 303.

Cumberland. (1) Between a cave in Italy and a moon-light lake in Cumberland. *M.P*.xvi. (2) " Les. C." in *L. & F.* 54.

Curtis, Mr. *Watsons*, 306.

D

Dalrymple, The Dowager Viscountess. *Pers.* xvi, xix.

Dalrymple, The late Viscount. Sir Walter had once been in company with the late Viscount, but had never seen any of the rest of the family. *Pers.* xvi.

D'Antraigues, Comte and Comtesse, visited by J. in 1811. *Life,* 250.

Danvers, with whom Louise Lesley left her husband and home. " Les. C." in *L. & F.* 47.

Daphne. *The Mystery* in *Mem.* iii.

Darcy, Fitzwilliam. Mr. Darcy soon drew the attention of the room by his fine, tall person, handsome features, noble mien, and the report . . . of his having ten thousand a year. *P.P.*iii.

Darcy, Georgiana, his sister. *P.P.*viii. Miss Darcy was tall and her appearance womanly and graceful. She was less handsome than her brother, but there was sense and good humour in her face, and her manners were perfectly unassuming and gentle. *P.P.*xliv.

Darcy, Lady Anne, *née* Fitzwilliam, mother of the two Darcys. You know of course, that Lady Catherine de Bourgh and Lady Anne Darcy were sisters. *P.P.* xvi.

Darcy, Mr., the late. His father, Miss Bennet, the late Mr. Darcy, was one of the best men that ever breathed. *P.P.*xvi.

Darkwood, Lady Bridget. " C. of L." in *L. & F.* 106.

Darling, Mrs. *Sand.* ix.

Dartford. I was last month at my friend Elliott's, near Dartford. *S.S.*xxxvi.

Dartford, the " Bull and George," whence J.A. wrote to C., October 24, 1798. *Life,* 109 ; *Lett.* i, 153.

Dashwood, Captain Henry. " C. of L." in *L. & F.* 108.

Dashwood, Mrs., his wife (see **Dashwood, Marianne**) *S.S.*i.

Dashwood, Elinor, eldest daughter of Henry. Elinor . . . possessed a strength of understanding and coolness of judgment which qualified her, though only nineteen, to be the counsellor of her mother. *S.S.*i.

Dashwood, Fanny, *née* Ferrars, John's wife. A strong caricature of [her husband]—more narrow-minded and selfish. *S.S.*i.

Dashwood, Harry, son of John and Fanny. *S.S.*i. We were obliged to take Harry to see the wild beasts at Exeter Exchange. *S.S.*xxxiii.

Dashwood Henry. *S.S.*i.

Dashwood, John, son of Henry Dashwood. He was not an ill-disposed young man, unless to be rather cold-hearted and rather selfish is to be ill-disposed. *S.S.*i.

Dashwood, Margaret, third daughter of Henry. A good-humoured, well-disposed girl. *S.S.*i.

Dashwood, Marianne, second daughter of Henry. Marianne's abilities were, in many respects, quite equal to Elinor's. She was sensible and clever, but eager in everything : her sorrows, her joys, could have no moderation. She was generous, amiable, interesting ; she was everything but prudent. The resemblance between her and her mother was strikingly great. *S.S.*i.

Davies, Dr. We came post all the way, and had a very smart beau to attend us. Dr. Davies was coming to town, and so we thought we'd join him in a post-chaise. *S.S.*xxxii.

Davis, Charlotte. The last two days he was always by the side of Charlotte Davis : I pitied his taste. *N.A.* xxvii.

Davis, Mrs., a visitor at Sanditon. *Sand.* vi.

Davison, T., Lombard Street, Whitefriars, London, the Printer of Vols. III and IV (*Persuasion*) of the first edition of *N.A.* and *Persuasion*, 1818.

Dawlish, Devon. (1) J.A. was there in 1802. *Life,* 173. (2) It seemed rather surprising to him that anybody could live in Devonshire without living near Dawlish. *S.S.*xxxvi.

Dawson, maid to Lady C. de Bourgh. Dawson does not object to the barouche-box. *P.P.*xxxvii.

Dawson, Miss. On Saturday we expect Miss Dawson to call in the Morning—which will complete my Daughter's Introduction into Life. " C. of L." in *L. & F.* 103.

Deal, Kent. The only time that I ever really suffered in body or mind. . . . was the winter that I passed by myself at Deal, when the Admiral . . . was in the North Seas. *Pers.* viii.

Deane, Hants., the parish of which, with Steventon, George Austen, J.'s father, was rector. A Deane woman was J.'s nurse.

D

Debary, Miss, who, wrote J.A., " is netting herself a gown in worsteds, and wears what Mrs. Birch would call a pot hat. A short and compendious history of Miss Debary ! " *Life,* 114.

Debary, Peter, who declined Deane curacy, because it was too far from London. *Life,* 158.

De Bourgh, Anne, *P.P.*xiv. The other is Miss de Bourgh. Only look at her. She is quite a little creature. Who would have thought she could be so thin and small ! *P.P.*xxviii.

De Bourgh, Lady Catherine, aunt to Darcy. *P.P.*xiii. Lady Catherine was a tall, large woman, with strongly marked features, which might once have been handsome. Her air was not conciliating . . . whatever she said was spoken in so authoritative a tone as marked her self-importance. *P.P.*xxix.

De Bourgh, Sir Lewis, deceased. *P.P.*xiii.

De Courcy, Lady, mother of Mrs. Vernon. *Lady S.* Lett. 3.

De Courcy, Reginald, her son. *Ibid,* Lett. 4.

De Courcy, Sir Reginald, her husband. *Ibid.* Lett. 12.

Delaford, Colonel Brandon's place. *S.S.*xiv. A nice, old-fashioned place, full of comforts and conveniences ; quite shut in with great garden walls that are covered with the best fruit-trees in the country ; and such a mulberry tree in one corner . . a dovecote, some delightful stewponds, and a very pretty canal. *S.S.*xxx.

Delaford Hanger. I have not seen such timber anywhere in Dorsetshire as there is now standing in Delaford Hanger ! *S.S.*l.

Delaford Parsonage. The parsonage is but a small one ... and very likely *may* be out of repair. *S.S.*xl.

Delamere, Frederic. " H. of E." in *L. & F.* 90, 93.

Denham, Esther, Sir Edward's sister, who lived with him. *Sand.* iii. Miss Denham was a fine young woman, but cold and reserved. *Sand.* vii.

Denham, Lady, *née* Brereton. The Great Lady of Sanditon ... a very rich old lady, who had buried two husbands [Mr. Hollis and Sir Harry Denham]. *Sand.* iii, vi.

Denham Park, the seat of Sir Edward Denham. *Ibid.* iii.

Denham Place, Sanditon. *Ibid.* iv.

Denham, Sir Edward, Bart., Sir Harry's nephew. *Ibid.* iii. Sir Edward was ... certainly handsome, but yet more to be remarked for his very good address and wish of paying attention and giving pleasure. *Ibid.* vii.

Denham, Sir Harry, Bart., deceased. *Ibid.* iii.

Denmark, Anne of. " H. of E." in *L. & F.* 94.

Dennison, Mrs., *S.S.*xxxvi.

Denny, Mr., an officer at Meryton. *P.P.*xiv, xv.

Derbyshire, (1) The county in which Darcy's Pemberley estate was situated. *P.P.*iii. (2) " C. of L." in *L. & F.* 115.

Devereux, Robert. *See* **Essex, Earl of.**

Devizes, (1) where the Austens were accustomed to break the journey (and stay a night) from Steventon to Bath. (2) *N.A.*xv.

Devonshire. A gentleman of consequence and property in Devonshire. *S.S.*iv.

Digweeds, The, two brothers who were the principal tenants at Steventon. References to them in the *Letters* are frequent.

Dixon, Mr. and Mrs. (*née* Campbell). *E.*xix.

Doge, The famous, at the Court of Lewis, xiv. *M.P.*xxii. When he was asked what he found most remarkable at Versailles, he replied—" C'est de m'y voir."

Donavan, an apothecary or doctor. *S.S.*xxxvii.

Donwell Abbey, Mr. Knightley's estate, in the parish of Donwell, adjoining Highbury. *E.*iii.

Donwell Lane, is never dusty. *E.*xlii.

Dorking. Let my accents swell to Mickleham on one side, and Dorking on the other. *E.*xliii.

Dorothea, Lady, the lady to whom Lindsay's father wished to give his son's hand. *L. & F.* 10, 13.

Dorothy, " the ancient housekeeper " of romances. *N.A.*xx.

Dorsetshire. (1) *S.S.*xxi. (2) *Pers.* xxii.

" Douglas," by Home, a quotation from—" My name was [is] Norval." *M.P.*xiii.

Dovedale, Derbyshire. The celebrated beauties of Matlock, Chatsworth, Dovedale, or the Peak. *P.P.* xlii.

Drake, Sir Francis. " H. of E." in *L. & F.* 93

Drawbridge, The, Portsmouth. They passed the Drawbridge, and entered the town. *M.P.*xxxviii.

Drayton, Dr. " C. of L." in *L. & F.* 115.

Drew, Sir Archibald and his grandson. There comes old Sir Archibald Drew and his grandson. Look, he sees us ; he kisses his hand to you ; he takes you for my wife. *Pers.* xviii.

Drummond, the maiden name of Mrs. Tilney. *N.A.*ix.

Drummond, Colonel and Mrs. " Les. C." in *L. & F.* 54, 55.

Drury Lane. *See* **London.**

Duberley, Lord [in Colman's *Heir at Law*]. *M.P.*xiv.

Dublin. *E.*xix.

Dugdale. *Pers.* i. The Elliot family was " mentioned in Dugdale." The reference is probably to Sir William Dugdale's *The Antient Usage in bearing of Arms, with catalogue of nobility and baronets of England, Scotland, Ireland.* 2nd. Ed., Oxford, 1682.

Dunbeath, the home of Lesley and his wife. " Les. C." in *L. & F.* 56

Dupuis, Mrs. Charles. *Sand.* ix

Durands, The. The little Durands . . . with their mouths open to catch the music ; like unfledged sparrows ready to be fed. *Pers.* xxi.

E

East, The. Or what did Sir Thomas think of Woolwich ? or how could a boy be sent out to the East ? *M.P.*i.

East Bourne. (1) *You* go to Brighton ! I would not trust you so near it as East Bourne for fifty pounds ! *P.P.*xlviii. (2) That part of the Sussex Coast which lies between Hastings and E. Bourne. *Sand.* i.

East Indies, The. (1) In the East Indies the climate is hot and the mosquitoes are troublesome. *S.S.*x. (2) William must not forget my shawl if he goes to the East Indies. *M.P.*xxxi. (3) He was in the Trafalgar action, and has been in the East Indies since. *Pers.* iii.

East Kingham Farm, " where old Gibson used to live." *S.S.*xxxiii.

Easton. The first day I went over Mansfield Wood, and Edmund took the copses beyond Easton, and we brought home six brace between us. *M.P.*xix.

Eastwell Park, near Godmersham, Kent, " where lived George Hatton and his wife Lady Elizabeth (*née* Murray) " ; visited by J. in 1805. *Lett.* i, 295, 298.

Ecclesford, Cornwall, Lord Ravenshaw's seat. *M.P.*xiii.

Edgar's Buildings. *See* **Bath.**

Edgeworth, Miss. *See* **Belinda.**

Edinburgh. (1) Edinburgh, where I hoped to find some kind, some pitying Friend. *L. & F.* 35. (2) " Les. C." in *L. & F.* 60.

Edward IV. " H. of E." in *L. & F.* 86.

Edward V. *Ibid.* 87.

Edward VI. *Ibid.* 89.

Edward Street. *See* **London.**

Edwards, Mr. *Watsons,* 298. Mr. Edwards lived in the best house in the street. *Ibid.* 309.

Edwards, Mrs. *Watsons,* 298. The mother though a very friendly woman, had a reserved air, and a great deal of formal civility. *Ibid.* 308.

Edwards, Mary, their daughter. I would advise you to ask Mary Edwards' opinion, if you are at all at a loss, for she has a very good taste. *Watsons,* 298, 308.

Egerton, T., Military Library, Whitehall [London], the publisher of the first editions of *Sense and Sensibility,* 3 vols., 1811 ; *Pride and Prejudice,* 3 vols., 1813 ; and *Mansfield Park,* 3 vols., 1814.

Elegant Extracts. He would read something aloud out of the *Elegant Extracts,* very entertaining. *E.iv. Elegant Extracts or useful and entertaining pieces of Poetry,* published in 1789.

" Elephant," The. Captain Walsh thinks you will certainly have a cruise to the westward, with the *Elephant. M.P.*xxxviii.

Elinor and Marianne. *See* **" Sense and Sensibility."**

Eliza. *See* **Brandon, Eliza.**

Eliza, the natural daughter of Mrs. Eliza Brandon. *See* **Williams.**

Elizabeth of York, who married Henry VII. " H. of E." in *L. & F.* 87

Elizabeth, Queen. (1) The house was built in Elizabeth's time. *M.P.*vi. (2) The destroyer of all comfort, the deceitful Betrayer of trust reposed in her, and the Murderess of her Cousin. " H. of E." in *L. & F.* 91.

Ellinor. Many have been the cares and vicissitudes of my past life, my beloved Ellinor. " Scraps " in *L. & F.* 136.

Elliot, Sir Walter, Bart., of Kellynch Hall, Somerset. Vanity was the beginning and the end of Sir Walter Elliot's character—vanity of person and of situation. He had been remarkably handsome in his youth, and, at fifty-four, was still a very fine man. *Pers.* i, iii.

Elliot, Lady, *née* Elizabeth Stevenson, deceased. Lady Elliot had been an excellent woman, sensible and amiable. *Pers.* i.

Elliot, Anne, their second daughter. Anne, with an elegance of mind and sweetness of character, which must have placed her high with any people of real understanding, was nobody with either father or sister. *Pers.* i, iii.

Elliot, Elizabeth, their eldest daughter. Elizabeth had succeeded, at sixteen, to all that was possible of her mother's rights and consequence ; and being very handsome, and very like himself [Sir Walter], her influence had always been great. *Pers.* i, iii.

Elliot, Mary, their third daughter. Mary had acquired a little artificial importance, by becoming Mrs. Charles Musgrove. *Pers.* i, v.

Elliot, William Walter, great grandson of the second Sir Walter and heir presumptive to Sir Walter Elliot. Instead of pushing his fortune in the line marked out for the heir of the house of Elliot, he had purchased independence by uniting himself to a rich woman of inferior birth. *Pers.* i, xii.

Elliot, Mrs., his wife. *Pers.* i. She was certainly not a woman of family, but well educated, accomplished, rich, and excessively in love with his friend [W. W. Elliot]. *Pers.* xv.

Elliott, Colonel and Fanny. *The Mystery* in *Mem.* iii.

Elliott, —, a friend of Robert Ferrars. I was last month at my friend Elliott's near Dartford. *S.S.*xxxvi.

Elliott, Lady, his wife. Lady Elliott wished to give a dance. *S.S.*xxxvi.

Ellis, Lady Bertram's maid. I suppose you would not think it fair to expect Ellis to wait on her as well as the others. *M.P.*i.

Ellison, Mr. and Mrs., guardians of Miss Grey. *S.S.*xxx.

Elton, Philip, Vicar of Highbury. *E.*i. Mr. Elton's being a remarkably handsome man, with most agreeable manners. *E.*vi.

Elton, Mrs., *née* Augusta Hawkins. *E.*xxi. Mrs. Elton was first seen at church : but though devotion might be interrupted, curiosity could not be satisfied by a bride in a pew, and it must be left for the visits in form which were then to be paid, to settle whether she were very pretty indeed, or only rather pretty, or not pretty at all. *E.*xxxii.

" Emma " was published in three volumes, 12 mo., price one guinea, by John Murray, in 1816. The name of the author was not given, but the title-page said it was " By the Author of *Pride and Prejudice*, etc." The novel had been begun in January, 1814, and was finished in March, 1815. The number of copies

printed was 2,000, of which 1,250 were sold within
the year (*Life*, 311). The second edition did not
appear till 1833.

Emmeline of Delamere, The. Elizabeth the torment
of Essex may be compared to the Emmeline of
Delamere. " H. of E." in *L. & F*. 93.

" Endymion," The, a ship at Portsmouth. *M.P*.xxxviii.

England. (1) Had I remained in England, perhaps . . .
S.S.xxxi. (2) How long ago it is, aunt, since we used
to repeat the chronological order of the kings of
England ? *M.P*.ii. (3) Beware of the insipid Vanities
and idle Dissipations of the Metropolis of England.
L. & F. 7. (4) " H. of E." in *L. & F*. 85. (5) He . . .
accused the laws of England for allowing them to
possess their Estates when wanted by their Nephews
or Nieces. " C. of L." in *L. & F*. 125.

Enscombe, Yorkshire, the home of the Churchills. *E*.ii.

Epsom. They removed into a hackney-coach, and
dismissed the chaise that brought them from Epsom.
P.P.xlvi.

Essex. Have you been long in Essex. Ma'am ? " C. of
L." in *L. & F*. 115.

Essex, Robert, Earl of. " H. of E." in *L. & F*. 90.

Eton. His leaving Eton for Oxford made no change
in his kind dispositions. *M.P*.ii.

Europe. My cousin cannot put the map of Europe
together. *M.P*.ii.

Evelyn, one of Jane's *Juvenilia*. *Life*, 55.

Evelyn, Mr. and Mrs. " C. of E." in *L. & F*. 114, 115.

Everingham, Norfolk, Henry Crawford's home. Everingham, as it *used* to be, was perfect in my estimation ;
such a happy fall of ground, and such timber ! *M.P.*vi.

Exeter. It [Barton Cottage] was within four miles
northward of Exeter. *S.S.*v.

Exeter Exchange. *See* **London.**

F

Fairfax, the Cromwellian general. " H. of E." in *L. & F.*
96.

Fairfax, Jane, (1). *See* the next article.

Fairfax, Jane, (2) the only child of Mrs. Bates's youngest
daughter, Jane, who married Lieut. Fairfax, and died
of consumption and grief soon after her husband was
killed. *E.*x. Jane Fairfax was very elegant . . . her
height was pretty . . . her figure particularly graceful ;
her size a most becoming medium . . . Her eyes, a
deep gray, with dark eyelashes and eyebrows, had
never been denied their praise ; but the skin . . .
had a clearness and delicacy which really needed no
fuller bloom. *E.*xx.

Fairfax, Lieutenant, of the — regiment of infantry, husband of Jane Fairfax (1). *E.*xx. He died in action
abroad.

Fanny, a cousin of Colonel Brandon. Perhaps it [a
letter] is to tell you that your cousin Fanny is married ?
*S.S.*xiii.

Faulkland, Viscount. " H. of E." in *L. & F.* 96.

Ferrars, Edward, brother of Mrs. John Dashwood. A gentlemanlike and pleasing young man . . . He was not handsome, and his manners required intimacy to make them pleasing. *S.S.*iii.

Ferrars, Mrs., mother of Edward and Robert. *S.S.*iii. Mrs. Ferrars was a little, thin woman, upright, even to formality, in her figure, and serious, even to sourness, in her aspect . . . a lucky contraction of the brow had rescued her countenance from the disgrace of insipidity, by giving it the strong characters of pride and ill-nature. *S.S.*xxxiv.

Ferrars, Robert, Edward's elder brother. *S.S.*xxii. [Silly, and a great coxcomb. *S.S.*xxiv.] xxxvi.

Ferrars, Sir Robert, uncle to Edward and Robert. *S.S.*xxxvi.

Feuillide, Jean Capotte, Comte de, married Miss Hancock (*q.v.*), a cousin of J.A.   On February 22, 1794, he was guillotined in the French Revolution. His widow married her cousin, Henry Austen (*q.v.*).

Feuillide, Eliza de, *née* Hancock. *See* the previous article.   To her J.A. inscribed her youthful production *Love and Freindship* (p. 4).

Fielding. *See* " **Tom Jones.**"

First Impressions. *See* "**Pride and Prejudice.**"

Fisher, Miss and Mrs. Jane, visitors at Sanditon. *Sand.* vi.

Fitzgerald, Susan, a friend of Charlotte Lutterell, *m.* Sir George Lesley.   " Les. C." in *L. & F.* 52, 53.

Fitzgerald, William, brother of Susan. *Ibid.* 61.

Fitzowen. " C. of L." in *L. & F.* 105.

Fitzwilliam, Colonel, nephew of Lady Catherine de Bourgh. Colonel Fitzwilliam, who led the way, was about thirty, not handsome, but in person and address most truly the gentleman. *P.P.*xxx.

Flambeau, Lady. Alas ! what Delightful Jewels will she be decked in this evening at Lady Flambeau's ! " Les. C." in *L. & F.* 78.

Fletcher, Sam, a friend of John Thorpe—who had a horse " to sell that would suit anybody." *N.A.*x.

Ford's. The principal woollen-draper, linen-draper, and haberdasher's shop united—the shop first in size and fashion [in Highbury]. *E.*xxi.

Ford, Mrs., proprietress of the shop. " No trouble in the world, ma'am," said the obliging Mrs. Ford. *E.*xxvii.

Fordyce's " Sermons," from which Mr. Collins read to the Bennet family—an inattentive audience. *P.P.*xiv. *Sermons to Young Women,* by James Fordyce, D.D., was published in 1766.

Forster, Colonel, in command of the Militia at Meryton, a dinner guest of Sir William Lucas. *P.P.*vi.

Forster, Harriet, his wife. Mrs. Forster promised to have a little dance in the evening (by the bye, Mrs. Forster and me are *such* friends !). *P.P.*xxxix.

Fortheringay [*sic*] **Castle.** She was executed in the Great Hall at Fortheringay Castle. (sacred Place !). " H. of E." in *L. & F.* 92.

Fowle, Charles, mentioned by J.A. in 1796. *Life,* 98.

Fowle, Eliza, *née* Lloyd, *m.* Fulwar Craven Fowle, lived at Kintbury, Berkshire, where J.A. visited them in 1816. *Mem.* xi.

Fowle, Fulwar Craven, Rector of Kintbury. *See* **Fowle, Eliza.**

Fowle, Thomas, brother of F. C. Fowle. He became engaged to J.'s sister, Cassandra, probably in 1795. He was then Rector of Allington, Wilts. *See* **Austen, Cassandra** (2).

France. (1) I was born in Spain and received my Education at a Convent in France. *L. & F.* 6. (2) He ... says that the air of France has greatly recovered both his Health and Spirits. " Les. C." in *L. & F.* 54. (3) His Majesty then turned his thoughts to France, where he went and fought the famous Battle of Agincourt. " H. of E." in *L. & F.* 85.

France, King of. *Ibid.* 88.

France, South of. Oh, that we had such weather here as they had at Udolpho, or at least in Tuscany and the South of France. *N.A.*xi.

Frankland, Mrs. I was looking after some window-curtains, which Lady Alicia and Mrs. Frankland were telling me of last night. *Pers.* xix.

Fraser, Mr. and Mrs. (*née* Janet Ross). *M.P.*xxxvi.

Fraser, Margaret, daughter of Mr. Fraser by his first wife, whom Mrs. Fraser " is wild to get married, and wants Henry to take." *M.P.*xxxvi.

Frasers, The Lady. He ... wished the Lady Frasers had been in the country. *N.A.*xxvi.

Frederick, a character in *Lovers' Vows* (*q.v.*).   *M.P.*xiv.

Freeman, an undergraduate of Christ Church, Oxford. *N.A.*vii.

Fullerton, the Wiltshire village where the Morlands lived.   *N.A.*i.

G

Gamester, The.   *M.P.*xiv.   *The Gamester*, by Edward Moore, was produced at Drury Lane, 1753.

Gardiner, Edward, Mrs. Bennet's brother.   *P.P.*ix. Mr. Gardiner was a sensible, gentlemanlike man, greatly superior to his sister, as well by nature as education.   *P.P.*xxv.

Gardiner, Mrs., his wife. Mrs. Gardiner . . . was an amiable, intelligent, elegant woman, and a great favourite with her Longbourn nieces.   *P.P.*xxv.

Garrick, David, and his charade. " Kitty, a fair but frozen maid."   *E.*ix.

Garrison Chapel, Portsmouth.   He was asked to go with them to the Garrison Chapel, which was exactly what he had intended.   *M.P.*xlii.

Gascoigne, Sir William. The King died, and was succeeded by his son Henry who had previously beat Sir William Gascoigne.   " H. of E." in *L. & F.* 85.

Gay.   *See* **Hare.**

Gay Street.   *See* **Bath.**

Genlis, Madame de, her *Adelaide and Theodore. E*.liii.
This English translation was published in 1783.

Giaour, The, [by Byron]. *Pers.* xi.

Gibraltar. (1) When Mrs. Brown, and the other women,
at the Commissioner's, at Gibraltar, appeared in the
same trim, I thought they were mad. *M.P*.xxiv ;
(2) where Dick Musgrove had been left ill. *Pers.* viii.

Gibraltar, Straits of. I never went beyond the Streights.
Pers. viii.

Gibson. East Kingham Farm . . . where old Gibson
used to live. *S.S.*xxxiii.

Gibson, Mary, first wife of Francis Austen (*q.v.*), whom
she married in 1806.

Gilbert, Mrs. and Miss. There will be the two Gilberts . . .
Somebody said that *Miss* Gilbert was expected at
her brother's, and must be invited with the rest.
Somebody else believed *Mrs.* Gilbert would have
danced the other evening, if she had been asked.
*E.*xxix.

Gilberts, The. It is very provoking that we should be
so few. Why did not you ask the Gilberts to come
to us to-day ? *S.S.*xx.

Gilpin, William : his *Tour of the Highlands. L. & F.* 37.
The allusion is to Gilpin's book, published in 1789,
with the long-winded title : *Observations, relative
chiefly to Picturesque Beauty, made in the year 1776,
on Several Parts of Great Britain; particularly the
High-Lands of Scotland.*

Gilpin, William. I would by no means pretend to

affirm that he was equal to those first of Men Robert Earl of Essex, Delamere, or Gilpin. "H. of E." in *L. & F.* 90. This comical reference would appear to be to the William Gilpin of the preceding article.

Glenford, Miss C. Lutterell's home. "Les. C." in *L. & F.* 49.

Gloucestershire, the county of the Tilney family. *N.A.*iii.

Godby, Miss. Miss Godby told Miss Sparks . . . *SS.*xxxviii.

Goddard, Mrs. The mistress of a school . . . a real, honest old-fashioned boarding-school. *E.*iii, xiii.

Godmersham Park, Kent, a residence of Thomas Knight (*q.v.*), later the property of Edward Austen, J.'s brother, who took the name of Knight. It is "in one of the most beautiful parts of Kent, namely, in the Valley of the Stour, which lies between Ashford and Canterbury." (*Lett.* i, 7). Mrs. Knight gave Edward Austen possession in 1798, in which year J.A. first visited Godmersham.

Goldsmith. (1) What Fanny told her of former times dwelt more on her mind than the pages of Goldsmith [i.e. Goldsmith's *History of England*]. *M.P.*xliii. (2) Goldsmith tells us that when lovely woman stoops to folly, she has nothing to do but to die. *E.*xlv. *See* also "**Vicar of Wakefield.**"

Goodnestone, near Wingham, Kent, the seat of Sir Brook Bridges, whose daughter Elizabeth married Edward Austen in 1791. J.A. visited it in 1805. (*Life,* 190.)

E

Goulding, William. We overtook William Goulding in his curricle. *P.P.*li.

Gower, Sir James. The approach of Sir James Gower (one of my too numerous admirers). "Les. C." in *L. & F.* 77.

Gracechurch Street. *See* **London.**

Graham, —, the husband proposed for Janetta by her father. Just such a man as one might have expected to be the choice of Macdonald. *L. & F.* 24.

Graham, Mr. I did not thoroughly understand what you were telling your brother . . . about your friend Mr. Graham's intending to have a bailiff from Scotland. *E.*xii.

"Grandison, Sir Charles" [by Samuel Richardson]. Mrs. Morland . . . very often reads *Sir Charles Grandison* herself ; but new books do not fall in our way. *N.A.*vi.

Grant, Rev. Dr., parson of Mansfield. *M.P.*iii.

Grant, Mrs., his wife, half-sister to Henry and Mary Crawford. The Doctor was very fond of eating, and would have a good dinner every day ; and Mrs. Grant, instead of contriving to gratify him at little expense, gave her cook as high wages as they did at Mansfield Park, and was scarcely ever seen in her offices. *M.P.*iii.

Grantley, Miss. I am quite in raptures with her beautiful little design for a table, and I think it infinitely superior to Miss Grantley's. *P.P.*x.

"Grappler," The, Captain Benwick's ship. He came home from the Cape—just made into the *Grappler*. *Pers.* xii.

Gray, the poet, quoted—" Many a flower " etc. *N.A.*i.

Gray's. *See* **London.**

Gray's Inn. *See* **London.**

Great Willingden, or **Willingden Abbots**—lies seven miles off, on the other side of Battel—quite down in the Weald. *Sand.* i.

Green, Mr. I was talking to Mr. Green at that very time about your mother's dairymaid. *M.P.*vii.

Green, Mr. From the accidental rencontre to the dinner at Mr. Green's. *E.*xxii.

Green Park Buildings. *See* **Bath.**

Gregory, Lucy—is courted by a lieutenant. *M.P.*xxv.

Gregorys, The—grown up amazing fine girls. *M.P.*xxv.

Grenville, Miss. " C. of L." in *L. & F.* 115.

Gretna Green. (1) Lydia's short letter . . . gave them to understand that they were going to Gretna Green. *P.P.*xlvi. (2) Sophia and I experienced the satisfaction of seeing them depart for Gretna Green, which they chose for the celebration of their Nuptials, in preference to any other place. *L. & F.* 26.

Greville, Ellen and Miss. Miss Greville laughed but I am sure Ellen felt for me. " C. of L." in *L. & F.* 110.

Greville, Lady. *Ibid.* 109.

Grey, Lady Jane. " H. of E." in *L. & F.* 88.

Grey, Sophia, whom Willoughby married. A smart, stylish girl, they say, but not handsome. [She had, however, £50,000.] *S.S.*xxx.

Grierson, Lady Mary, and her daughters. If you had been a week later at Lisbon . . . you would have been asked to give a passage to Lady Mary Grierson and her daughters. *Pers.* viii.

Griffiths, Mrs., and her family. *Sand.* ix, xi.

Grosvenor Street. *See* **London.**

Guildford. Just now it is a sickly time at Guildford. *Watsons,* 360.

Gustavus, a grandson of Lord St. Clair (*q.v.*). *L. & F.* 22.

H

Haden, Mr., " the apothecary from the corner of Sloane Street." (J.'s letter to C., October 17, 1815.) Mr. Haden was " the father of Sir Seymour Haden, and the introducer into England of the stethoscope " (*Life,* 309n). He attended Henry Austen during his illness in October, 1815, and dined with J.A. on November 25, 1815. (*Life,* 315.)

Haggerston, a lawyer. I will immediately give directions to Haggerston for preparing a proper settlement. *P.P.*xlix.

Hailsham, Sussex. *Sand.* i.

Halton, Henrietta—a young lady very much in love. " C. of L." in *L. & F.* 119.

Hamilton, Miss. *See* **Smith, Mrs.**

Hamiltons, The. It was the same when I wanted to join the Hamiltons to the Lakes. *Lady S.*, Lett. 28.

"Hamlet." (1) *SS*.xvi. (2) *M.P.*xiv. There is also an allusion in xiii—How many a time have we . . . *to be'd* and *not to be'd* in this very room for his amusement !

Hampden. " H. of E." in *L. & F.* 96.

Hampshire. A long journey from Hampshire taken for nothing. *Sand.* xi.

Hancock, Eliza, daughter of **Philadelphia Hancock** (*q.v.*). She was educated in Paris, and married (1) the Comte de Feuillide (*q.v.*), (2) in December 1797, her first cousin Henry Austen, Jane's third brother.

Hancock, Philadelphia, *née* Austen, a sister (one of two) of J.A.'s father. She married Tysoe Saul Hancock, surgeon, at Cuddalore, India, on February 22, 1753, and " died in the winter of 1791–2." (*Life*, 43.) Her husband died in November, 1775.

Hancock, Tysoe Saul. *See* the preceding article.

Hanking, Rev. Mr., a visitor at Sanditon. *Sand.* vi.

Hannah, housemaid at Randalls, and daughter of James, the Woodhouses' coachman. *E.*i.

Hanover Square. *See* **London.**

Hans Place. *See* **London.**

Harding, Dr. It is a rich old Dr. Harding, uncle to the friend she goes to see. *Watsons*, 301.

Harding, Mr., " an old and most particular friend "
of Sir Thomas Bertram. *M.P.*xlvii.

" Hare and Many Friends, The," (from Gay's *Fables*)
mentioned *N.A.*i. ; quoted (" For when a lady's in
the case, you know, all other things give place.")
*E.*lii.

Harley Street. *See* **London.**

Harpsden, near Henley-upon-Thames, of which Thomas
Leigh, Jane's grandfather, was rector.

Harrington, Harriet and Pen. She asked the two
Harringtons to come : but Harriet was ill, and so
Pen was forced to come by herself. *P.P.*xxxix.

Harris, Mr., the Palmers' apothecary. *S.S.*xliii.

Harrison, Colonel. *M.P.*xxix.

Harry, Mr. Knightley's man-servant. I am sure I would
not have such a creature as his Harry stand at our
side-board for any consideration. *E.*lii.

Hartfield, the home of the Woodhouses at Highbury.
*E.*i.

Harville, Captain. *Pers.* viii. Captain Harville was a
tall, dark man, with a sensible, benevolent countenance ; a little lame. *Pers.* xi.

Harville, Mrs., his wife. *Pers.* viii. Mrs. Harville, a
degree less polished than her husband, seemed,
however, to have the same good feelings. *Pers.* xi.

Harville, Fanny, the captain's sister, had been engaged
to Captain Benwick. Fanny Harville did not live to
know it. She had died the preceding summer, while
he was at sea. *Pers.* xi.

Harwoods, The, neighbours of the Austens at Steventon. J.A. dined with them in January, 1799, also danced with " J. Harwood, who I think takes to me rather more than he used to do." (*Life*, 122, 123.)

Hastings. That part of the Sussex Coast which lies between Hastings and E. Bourne. *Sand.* i.

Hatfield. Making every possible inquiry . . . at the inns in Barnet and Hatfield, but without any success. *P.P.*xlvi.

Hatton, George and Lady Elizabeth, of Eastwell Park, near Godmersham, Kent, visited by J.A. in 1805. *Lett.* i, 295, 298.

Hawkins, Augusta, " the youngest of the two daughters of a Bristol-merchant, of course, he must be called," who married Mr. Elton. *See* **Elton, Mrs.**

Hawkins. Selina, her sister, who married Mr. Suckling. *See* **Suckling, Mrs.**

Haye Park, near Longbourn, where the Gouldings lived. *P.P.*l.

Hayter, Charles, cousin of the Musgroves. Charles Hayter was . . . a very amiable, pleasing young man . . . He was in orders. *Pers.* ix.

Hayter, Mr. Mr. Hayter had some property of his own, but it was insignificant compared with Mr. Musgrove's. *Pers.* ix.

Hayter, Mrs., his wife. Mrs. Musgrove and Mrs. Hayter were sisters. They had each had money. *Pers.* ix.

Hayters, the Miss, the females of the family of cousins already mentioned. *Pers.* viii.

Heartley, Mr., mentioned by J., 1796. *Life,* 99.

Heathcote, Miss, mentioned by J., 1796. *Life,* 98.

Heathcote, Mrs., *née* Elizabeth Bigg, who, with her sister, Alethea Bigg " did all they could to promote the comfort of the sisters," Cassandra and Jane, during J.A.'s last illness at Winchester. (*Mem.* xi.) Mrs. Heathcote and her sister lived in the Close, Winchester.

Heeley, William. Look at William Heeley's windows— Blue Shoes and nankin Boots !—Who would have expected such a sight at a Shoemaker's in old Sanditon ! *Sand.* iv.

" Heir at Law, The " [by George Colman]. *M.P.*xiv.

Hemming, Mr. Mr. Marshall and Mr. Hemming change their dress every day of their lives before dinner. *Watsons,* 351.

Hendon, where J. A. visited Ben Lefroy (*q.v.*) and his wife (her niece Anna) in 1814. *Life,* 308.

Henrietta Street. *See* **London.**

Henry —, Sir. Sir Henry thought the duke not equal to Frederick, but that was because Sir Henry wanted the part himself. *M.P.*xiii.

Henry IV. Henry the 4th ascended the throne of England much to his own satisfaction. " H. of E." in *L. & F.* 85.

Henry V. *Ibid.* 85.

Henry VI. I cannot say much for this Monarch's sense. *Ibid.* 86.

Henry VII. This monarch soon after his accession married the Princess Elizabeth of York, by which alliance he plainly proved that he thought his own right inferior to hers, tho' he pretended to the contrary. *" H. of E."* in *L. & F.* 86.

Henry VIII. The Crimes and Cruelties of this Prince were too numerous to be mentioned. *Ibid.* 88.

" Henry VIII," Shakespeare's. I once saw Henry the Eighth acted. *M.P.*xxxiv.

Henry, Prince, eldest son of James I. *" H. of E."* in *L. & F.* 94.

" Henry and Eliza," an early sketch. *Life,* 57.

" Henry and Emma," by Prior, an allusion to. Without emulating the feelings of our Emma towards her Henry, she would have attended on Louisa with a zeal above the common claims of regard, for his sake. *Pers.* xii.

Henshawe, Biddy, aunt to Miss Grey. I remember her aunt very well, Biddy Henshawe ; she married a very wealthy man. *S.S.*xxx.

Hereford. (1) We are going to Lord Longtown's, near Hereford, for a fortnight. *N.A.*xxviii. (2) We each . . . hopped home from Hereford delightfully. *" Scraps "* in *L. & F.* 138.

Hermitage Walk. *See* **Bath.**

Hertfordshire, the county of Longbourn village and Netherfield Park. *P.P.*iii.

Hervey, Diana, Henry Hervey's aunt. Mrs. Diana . . . is

a professed enemy to everything which is not directed by Decorum and Formality. "Les. C." in *L. & F.* 69.

Hervey, Henry. Hervey had been thrown from his Horse, had fractured his Scull. *Ibid.* 50.

Heywood, Mr. A well-looking Hale, Gentlemanlike Man of middle age. *Sand.* i.

Heywood, Mrs., his wife. *Sand.* ii.

Heywood, Charlotte, their eldest daughter. A very pleasing young woman of two-and-twenty. *Sand.* ii.

Highbury, "the large and populous village, almost amounting to a town," the scene of the story. *E.*i.

Highchurch Down. Almost every day since they first met on Highchurch Down. *S.S.*xii.

High Street, Portsmouth. They passed the Drawbridge, and . . . were rattled into a narrow street, leading from the High Street. *M.P.*xxxviii.

Hill, Mrs. Mrs. Bennet's housekeeper. *P.P.*xiii, xlix.

Hill Street. *See* **London.**

Hillier, Mr. It is an honest old Place—and Hillier keeps it in very good order. *Sand.* iv.

Hillier, Mrs., his wife. Mrs. Hillier . . . did not seem at all aware of the Wind being anything more than common. *Sand.* iv.

"History of England, The," "from the reign of Henry the 4th to the death of Charles the 1st. By a partial, prejudiced, and ignorant historian." The end is dated "Saturday, November 26th, 1791," when the author was not quite sixteen years of age. It is

dedicated to the author's sister " with all due respect " ; and the Note is added : " N.B.—There will
be very few dates in this History." The manuscript
was illustrated by a series of medallion " portraits "
of the monarchs, in colours, by the author's sister,
Cassandra. The " History " was printed for the
first time, with other Juvenilia, in *Love and Freindship*,
1922, pp. 81–97. The " portraits " were reproduced
on the end-papers of the volume.

Hoare, Prince. *See* **My Grandmother.**

Hodges, Charles, who, said Isabella Thorpe, " will
plague me to death, I dare-say ; but I shall cut him
very short." *N.A.*xvi.

Hodges, Mrs., Mr. Knightley's housekeeper. For Mrs.
Hodges *would* be cross sometimes. *E.*xxvii.

Holborn. *See* **London.**

Holder, Mrs. and Miss, Bath acquaintances. *Life.*
169, 170.

Holford, Mrs. I met her at Mrs. Holford's, and did not
recollect her. *M.P.*v.

Hollis, Mr., first husband of Miss Bereton, afterwards
Lady Denham. *Sand.* iii.

Holyhead. The Campbells leave town in their way
to Holyhead the Monday following. *E.*xix.

Home, John. *See* **Douglas.**

Honiton, Devon. *S.S.* xiii.

"Horrid Mysteries." *N.A.*vi. By Peter Will, published
in 1796.

Hotel, The, Sanditon. In this row were . . . a little detached from it, the Hotel and Billiard Room. *Sand* iv.

Hounslow. " Scraps " in *L. & F.* 134.

House of Commons, The. (1) They must have been seen together . . . twice in the lobby of the House of Commons. *Pers.* i. (2) He . . . wished *he* were in the House of Commons, that he might reform the Legislature, and rectify all its abuses. " C. of L." in *L. & F.* 125.

Howard, Mr. . . . formerly tutor to Lord Oxborne, now clergyman of the parish in which the Castle stood. *Watsons,* 317.

Hughes, Dr., Mrs., and Richard. Ah ! Dr. Hughes, I declare . . . and Miss Hughes . . . where's dear Mrs. Richard ? *E.*xxxviii.

Hughes, Mrs. A request . . . that she would move a little to accommodate Mrs. Hughes and Miss Tilney with seats. *N.A.*viii.

Humbug, Old, Young and Mrs. *The Mystery* in *Mem.* iii.

Hume, the historian. *N.A.*xiv.

Hunsford, near Westerham, Kent, the parish of which the Rev. William Collins was rector, and the Rt. Hon. Lady Catherine de Bourgh, patron. *P.P.*xiii.

Hunt, Captain, an acquaintance of Isabella Thorpe. *N.A.*vi.

Hunter, Captain. Only observe whether she dances with Captain Hunter more than once—I have my fears in that quarter. *Watsons,* 305, 316.

Huntingdon. Lady Bertram was a " Miss Maria Ward, of Huntingdon." *M.P.*i.

Hurst, Mr. Mr. Hurst merely looked the gentleman. *P.P.*iii.

Hurst, Louisa, his wife, and sister of Mr. Bingley. *P.P.*iii.

Hurst and Wilford. I have dined with him at Hurst and Wilford. *Lady S.*, Lett 4.

Hurstbourne, Hants, a ball at, attended by J.A. *Life* 150.

I

Ibbotsons, The. The Ibbotsons—were they there ? *Pers.* xxi.

Ibthorp, where Mrs. and the Miss Lloyds lived. *See* **Lloyd.** Ibthorp was eighteen miles from Steventon. J.A. paid more than one visit there.

"Idler, The," [by Dr. Johnson]. Here are Crabbe's *Tales*, and the *Idler*, at hand to relieve you. *M.P.*xvi.

Ireland. (1) We asked her . . . which way she would go to get to Ireland ; and she said, she should cross to the Isle of Wight. *M.P.*ii. (2) The case is, you see, that the Campbells are going to Ireland. *E.*xix. (3) No letter of condolence had been sent to Ireland. *Pers.* xvi. (4) She is gone to settle in Ireland. I do not wonder that you should not wish to go with her into *that* country. *Watsons*, 313.   (5) My father was a native of Ireland, and an inhabitant of Wales. *L. & F.* 6.   (6) " H. of E." in *L. & F.* 94.

Isabel, one of the correspondents in *Love and Freindship.* *L. & F.* 5.

Isle of Wight.   (1) She thinks of nothing but the Isle of Wight, and she calls it *the Island,* as if there were no other island in the world.   *M.P.*ii.   (2) The far-famed Isle of Wight.   *Pers.* xi.   (3) I . . . conclude his scheme to the I. of Wight has not taken place. *Sand.* v.

" Italian, The," [by Ann Radcliffe].   When you have finished Udolpho, we will read the *Italian* together. *N.A.*vi.

Italy.   (1) Where Tintern Abbey held its station between a cave in Italy and a moonlight lake in Cumberland.   *M.P.*xvi.   (2) *N.A.*xxv.   (3) " Les. C." in *L. & F.* 54.

J

" Jack and Alice," an early sketch.   *Life,* 57.

Jackson, an undergraduate of Oriel, Oxford.   *N.A.*vii.

Jackson, Christopher.   The carpenter's work may be all done at home by Christopher Jackson himself. *M.P.*xiii.

Jackson, Dick, his son.   *M.P.*xv.

ackson, Eleanor, daughter of Henry Jackson, of London. In 1820 she became the second wife of Henry Austen (*q.v.*).

Jackson, Henry. *See* the preceding article.

James, a servant who waited on the Austens at Lyme in 1804. *Life*, 178.

James, Mr. Woodhouse's coachman. James will not like to put the horses to for such a little way. *E*.i.

James, a servant of the Watsons. *Watsons*, 304.

James, Reginald de Courcy's servant. *Lady S.*, Lett. 23.

James I. Though this King had some faults . . . I cannot help liking him. " H. of E." in *L. & F.* 94.

James II. This chapel was fitted up as you see it in James the Second's time. *M.P.*ix.

Jane, Miss, sister-in-law to Lady B. Darkwood. " C. of L." in *L. & F.* 106.

Janetta. *See* **Macdonald.**

Jebb's, a shop at Sanditon. *Sand.* iv.

Jeffereys, Mrs—Clara Partridge that was. *E*.xxxii.

Jefferies, Mrs. I . . . had promised John Groom to write to Mrs. Jefferies about his son. *M.P.*vii.

Jemima, the Musgroves' maid at Uppercross Cottage. If Jemima were not the trustiest, steadiest creature in the world . . . *Pers.* vi.

Jenkinson, Mrs., companion to Lady C. de Bourgh and her daughter. *P.P.*xix, xxviii.

Jennings, Mr., deceased. *S.S.*xi. How fond he was of it ! [old Constantia wine.] Whenever he had a touch of his old colicky gout, he said it did him more good than anything else in the world. *S.S.*xxx.

Jennings, Mrs., his widow, Lady Middleton's mother. A good-humoured, merry, fat, elderly woman, who talked a great deal, seemed very happy, and rather vulgar. *S.S.*vii.

Jenny, a maid of the Austens at Lyme, 1804. *Life,* 178, 179.

Joan of Arc. It was in this reign that Joan of Arc lived and made such a *row* among the English. " H. of E." in *L. & F.* 86.

John, servant to Mrs. Collins. You must send John with the young ladies, Mrs. Collins. *P.P.*xxxvii.

John, servant to the Gardiners. *P.P.*xlvi.

John, a groom, mentioned by Mrs. Norris as " John Groom." *M.P.*vii.

Johnson, Alicia, a friend of Lady Susan. *Lady S.,* Lett. 2.

Johnson, Mr., her husband. If I am as little in favour with Mr. Johnson as ever, you must come to me. *Lady S.,* Lett. 2.

Johnson, Dr. Samuel. (1) His " celebrated judgment as to matrimony and celibacy." *M.P.*xxxix. This was —" Marriage has many pains, but celibacy has no pleasures." *Rasselas,* ch. xxvi. (2) We shall be over-powered with Johnson and Blair all the rest of the way. *N.A.*xiv. (3) *See also* "**Idler**" and "**Rambler.**"

Johnson, Elizabeth and Fanny. " Scraps " in *L. & F.* 138.

Jones, Mr., apothecary. They insist also on my seeing Mr. Jones. *P.P.*vii.

Jones, Philip, a bricklayer, reputed father of Philander. *L. & F.* 39.

Julius Cæsar. How many a time have we mourned over the dead body of Julius Cæsar . . . in this very room for his amusement ! *M.P.*xiii.

K

Kellynch, Somerset, the village where the Elliots lived. *Pers.* i.

Kellynch Hall, Sir Walter Elliot's residence. *Pers.* i.

Kenilworth. *P.P.*xlii.

Kensington Gardens. *See* **London.**

Kent, (1) the county of Hunsford, near Westerham. *P.P.*xiii. (2) It is impossible to say when you may see him in Kent. *Lady S.*, Lett. 8.

Kentish Gazette. These advertisements, which I cut out myself from the Morning Post and the Kentish Gazette. *Sand.* i.

Keppel Street. *See* **London.**

Keynsham. They . . . were within view of the town of Keynsham. *N.A.*xi.

Kickabout, The Hon. Mrs. I accompanied Lady Lesley to a Rout at the Honourable Mrs. Kickabout's. "Les. C." in *L. & F.* 77.

King, Mary (Miss). *P.P.*iii.

F

King, Mr., who introduced Henry Tilney to Catherine Morland. *N.A.*iii. James King, M.C. of the Lower Rooms at Bath, 1785 : M.C. of the Upper Rooms, 1805.

King, The, in *Henry VIII.* *M.P.*xxxiv.

King's Bench, The. " C. of L." in *L. & F.* 112.

Kingsdown, near Bath, to which J.A. drove. *Life,* 171.

Kingston, Surrey. He is sure to ride through [Highbury] every week in his way to Kingston. *E.*iv.

King's-Weston. (1) We explored to King's-Weston twice last summer. *E.*xxxii. (2) We shall drive directly to Clifton and dine there ; and . . . if there is time for it go on to Kingsweston. *N.A.*xi.

Kintbury, Berkshire, where the Fowles (*q.v.*) lived— visited by J.A. in 1816. *Life,* 234.

" Kitty, a fair but frozen maid," by Garrick. *E.*ix.

Kitty or the Bower, an early fragment. *Life,* 55, 56.

Knatchbull, Catherine,   *m.* Thomas Knight. They adopted Edward Austen, to whom Mr. Knight left Godmersham Park and Chawton House. There is an allusion to Mrs. Knight in the " H. of E." in *L. & F.* 92.   *See* **Austen, Edward,** and **Knight, Thomas.**

Knatchbull, Fanny Catherine.   *See* **Knight, Fanny Catherine.**

Knight, Catherine.   *See* **Knatchbull, Catherine.**

Knight, Fanny Catherine, *b.* January 23, 1793, eldest daughter of Edward Austen (*q.v.*) who took the name of Knight in 1812. She married Sir Edward Knatchbull on October 24, 1820, and died December 25, 1882.

Their son, the first Lord Brabourne, published and edited J.A.'s *Letters*, 2 vols., 1884.

Knight, George, son of Edward Austen (Knight)—the " itty Dardy " of a letter of J.'s in 1798. He became " a well-known Kent cricketer, and one of the principal agents in the introduction of round-arm bowling." (*Life*, iii n.)

Knight, Thomas, of Godmersham Park, Kent, and Chawton House, Hampshire, a cousin of J.A. He adopted Edward Austen (*q.v.*) and bequeathed him his properties. He died in 1794—*See Lett.* i, 9, 10. He married Catherine Knatchbull (*q.v.*). They had no issue.

Knightley, George, of Donwell Abbey. A sensible man about seven or eight and thirty. *E.*i.

Knightley, John, his younger brother. *E.*v. Mr. John Knightley was a tall, gentleman-like, and very clever man ; rising in his profession, domestic and respectable in his private character ; but with reserved manners . . . . and capable of being sometimes out of humour. *E.*xi.

Knightley, Isabella, *née* Woodhouse, his wife. *E.*i. Mrs. John Knightley was a pretty, elegant little woman, of gentle, kind manners, and a disposition remarkably amiable and affectionate. *E.*xi.

Knightley, Henry, John, Bella, and George, their children. *E.*vi and xiii.

Knightley, Emma, their youngest child. A nice little girl about eight months old. *E.*xii.

Kympton, a village near Pemberley. *P.P.*lii.

L

"**Laconia,**" **The,** Captain Wentworth's ship, on which Richard Musgrove was for six months a midshipman. *Pers.* vi.

Lady of Branxholm Hall. *See* "**Lay of the Last Minstrel.**"

"**Lady of the Lake**" [by Scott]. *Pers.* xi.

"**Lady Susan,**" a complete short story, written about 1805, and first published in 1871, as an appendix to the second edition of J. E. Austen-Leigh's *Memoir of Jane Austen.* The MS. was given, probably by Cassandra Austen, to her niece, Lady Knatchbull (the Fanny Knight of the *Letters*), and it was by her permission printed in 1871. It is written in the form of letters.

Lake District, The, (1) to which Elizabeth Bennet was going on tour with the Gardiners. *P.P.*xlii. (2) It was the same, when I wanted to join the Hamiltons to the Lakes. *Lady S.,* Lett. 28.

Lambe, Miss, who had " an immense fortune . . . and very delicate health." *Sand.* ix.

Lambton, Derbyshire. The little town of Lambton, the scene of Mrs. Gardiner's former residence. *P.P.*xlii.

Lancastrians, The. There were several Battles between the Yorkists and Lancastrians, in which the former (as they ought) usually conquered. " H. of E." in *L. & F.* 86.

Land's End, The. The noblest expanse of Ocean between the South foreland and the Land's end. *Sand.* iv.

Langham. I was telling you of my idea of moving the path to Langham. *E.*xii.

Lansdown Crescent, Hill and **Road.** *See* **Bath.**

Langford, the home of the Manwaring's. *Lady S.,* Lett. i.

Larkins, William, Mr. Knightley's bailiff. The very same evening William Larkins came over with a large basket of apples. *E.*xxvii.

Larolles, Miss. The inimitable Miss Larolles. *Pers.* xx. This lady was a character in Fanny Burney's *Cecilia* —*See* Bk. IV, ch. ii.

Lascelles, Lady, former owner of the Rushworths' house in Wimpole Street. *M.P.*xl.

Lathom, Francis. *See* **Midnight Bell.**

Latournelle, Mrs. Jane and Cassandra Austen were at her school—the Abbey School in the Forbury, Reading —for a short time. (*Mem.* i.)

Laud, Archbishop. " H. of E." in *L. & F.* 96.

Laura, one of the correspondents in *Love and Freindship*. *L. & F.* 5.   Cf. **St. Clair.**

Laura Place. *See* **Bath.**

Laurina, an Italian opera-girl. *See* **St. Clair.**

" Lay of the last Minstrel," by Scott. (1) Here are . . . no banners, cousin, to be " blown by the night wind of heaven." No signs that a " Scottish monarch sleeps below." [See *Lay,* ii, 12.] *M.P.*ix. (2) Stopping

at the entrance door like the Lady of Branxholm
Hall, " one moment and no more " [See *Lay* i, 20.]
*M.P.*xxviii.

Layton's. *See* **London.**

Lee, Miss, governess in the family of Sir Thomas Bertram.
It will be just the same to Miss Lee, whether she has
three girls to teach, or only two. *M.P.*i.

Lefroy, Benjamin, son of Mr. Lefroy (*q.v.*)   He married
Anne Austen in November 1814. J.A., writing to
her in that month, said jestingly—" I dare say your
husband was in love with me once, and would never
have thought of you if he had not supposed me dead
of a scarlet fever." (*Mem.* v.)

Lefroy, Lucy, is mentioned in J.A.'s letter to her sister
dated April 21, 1805—" whose gracious manners,
ready wit, and solid remarks, put me somewhat in
mind of my old acquaintance, L.L." (*Mem.* iv).
In another letter, of April 8, 1805, J.A. says : " Seven
years and four months ago we went to the same
riding-house [at Bath] to see Miss Lefroy's perfor-
mance ! " (*Mem.* iv.)

Lefroy, Mr., was rector of Ashe, a parish adjoining
Steventon.

Lefroy, Mrs., his wife, sister to Sir Egerton Brydges.
The little Jane was very intimate with her. She is
mentioned in J.'s juvenile " History of England " (*L. &
F.* 92.)   She was killed by a fall from her horse on
December 16, 1804. (*Mem.* iii.)

Lefroy, Thomas, a nephew of Mrs. Lefroy, an intimate
acquaintance of Jane for a short time in early life.

They became acquainted in 1795–6, met at various dances, and indulged in some flirtation. He married in 1799 and became Chief Justice of Ireland, but never forgot Jane. (*Life*, 88, 89.)

Leicester Abbey, the " father Abbott of." " H. of E." in *L. & F.* 88.

Leicestershire. Fletcher and I mean to get a house in Leicestershire against the next season. *N.A.*x.

Leigh, Cassandra (1), daughter of Theophilus Leigh (*q.v.*) She married Samuel Cooke, Rector of Little Bookham, Surrey, who was J.A.'s godfather. They and their three children, Theophilus, Mary and George, all formed part of the circle of early friends of J. and her parents. (*Life*, 19.)

Leigh, Cassandra (2), youngest daughter of Thomas Leigh (*q.v.*). She married George Austen in 1764, and became J.'s mother. *See* **Austen, Cassandra** (1) and **Austen, George** (1).

Leigh, James, afterwards James Leigh Perrot. *See* **Perrot.**

Leigh, Jane, daughter of Thomas and sister of James Leigh and of J.A.'s mother. She married Edward Cooper (*q.v.*), and died in 1783.

Leigh, Dr. Theophilus, Master of Balliol College, Oxford, for more than fifty years, was uncle of J.A.'s mother —a man " more famous for his sayings than his doings, overflowing with puns and witticisms and sharp retorts." (*Mem.* i.)

Leigh, Thomas, Rector of Harpsden, near Henley-upon-

Thames, father of Cassandra (J.A.'s mother), Jane and James. He died in 1763.

" Lesley Castle," a fragment, described as " An unfinished Novel in Letters," which was first printed in the *Love and Freindship* volume, 1922 (pp. 43–79). It is dedicated to " Henry Thomas Austen Esqre," by his " obliged humble Servant the Author," and to the Dedication is appended the mock order : " Messrs. Demand and Co. please to pay Jane Austen, Spinster the sum of one hundred guineas on account of your Humble Servant H. T. Austen."

Lesley Castle. Our old and Mouldering Castle, which is situated two miles from Perth on a bold projecting Rock. " Les. C." in *L. & F.* 47.

Lesley, Family, The. Mr. Lesley ; Louisa Lesley (*née* Burton) his wife ; Sir George Lesley, his father ; Margaret and Matilda Lesley—all in *Ibid.* 47. Louisa Lesley, the little daughter of Mr. and Mrs. Lesley, *Ibid.* 48. Susan Lesley (*née* Fitzgerald), the wife of Sir George. *Ibid.* 53.

Lessingby. Those five or six days more at Lessingby might have been felt all my life ! *M.P.*xxxv.

Lewis, M.G. *See* **Monk, The.**

Lewis XIV. I am something like the famous Doge at the court of Lewis XIV. [See **Doge.**] *M.P.*xii.

Limehouse. *See* **London.**

Lindsay, Augusta, sister to Edward. I found her exactly what her Brother had described her to be—of the middle size. *L. & F.* 12.

Lindsay, Edward, son of Sir Edward and brother of Augusta. The noble youth informed us that his name was Lindsay—for particular reasons however I shall conceal it under that of Talbot. *L. & F.* 9.

Lindsay, Sir Edward, father of Edward and Augusta. My Father (he considered) is a mean and mercenary wretch. *L. & F.* 10, 14.

Lion, The, an inn room. " Scraps " in *L. & F.* 133.

Lisbon. *Pers.* viii.

Little, Captain, of Limehouse, a visitor at Sanditon. *Sand.* vi.

Little Bookham. *See* **Leigh, Cassandra** (1).

Little Theatre, The. *See* **London.**

Liverpool, (1) where Mary King lived. *P.P.*xxxix. (2) *M.P.*xix.

Liverpool Museum. *See* **London.**

Lloyd, Eliza, sister of Martha and Mary Lloyd, *m.* Fulwar Craven Fowle. *See* **Fowle.**

Lloyd, Martha, an early friend of J.A. She came to live with Mrs. Austen and her daughters, on the death of her mother in 1805. She lived with them till after Mrs. Austen's death in 1827. (*Life*, 188.) She married Francis Austen (*q.v.*) as his second wife in 1828, and died in 1843.

Lloyd, Mary, sister of Eliza and Martha. She married J.'s eldest brother, James Austen (*q.v.*) as his second wife, in 1797, and became the mother of James Edward Austen-Leigh, author of the *Memoir*, and his sister Caroline. She died in 1843.

Lodge, The, Kellynch, Lady Russell's residence. *Pers.* xiii.

London. (1) Mrs. Smith has this morning exercised the privilege of riches upon a poor dependent cousin, by sending me on business to London. *S.S.*xv. (2) The idea of his being gone to London only to get a large party for the ball. *P.P.*iii. (3) This will not do seventy miles from London. *M.P.*vi. (4) Her sister . . . being settled in London, only sixteen miles off. *E.*i. (5) She could compare . . . its [Bath's] fashions with the fashions of London. *N.A.*iv. (6) She travelled up to London with her father, for a few weeks' annual enjoyment of the great world. *Pers.* i. (7) I shall go through London, where I have business. *Lady S.*, Lett. 23. (8) We are on our road home from London. *Sand.* i. (9) He had been in London and was now on his way home. *Watsons*, 353. (10) What probability is there of my ever tasting the Dissipations of London ? *L. & F.* 7. (11) " Les. C." in *L. & F.* 49. (12) The King's riding through the streets of London with Anna Bullen. " H. of E." in *L. & F.* 89.   (13) " Scraps " in *L. & F.* 133.

London : Localities.

1. **Astley's,** (1) where J.A. went in August 1796. *Life*, 100, *Lett.* i, 134. (2) *E.*liv. This was the improved house known as " The Royal Saloon, or Astley's Amphitheatre." " The entertainment, at first, was only a day exhibition of horsemanship. Transparent fire-works, slack-rope vaulting . . . were subsequently added, the ride enlarged, and the house opened in the evening " (Wheatley,

London i, 76.) It had been burned down in 1794, was burned again in 1803, and yet again in 1841. There is a description of Astley's, at a date some forty years later than J.A.'s visit, in Dickens's *Sketches by Boz*.

2. **Baker Street.** The Andersons of Baker Street. *M.P.*v.

3. **Bank, The.** *N.A.*xiv.

4. **Bartlett's Buildings,** Holborn, where the Miss Steeles' cousin lived. *S.S.*xxxii. These Buildings were " named after Thomas Bartlett, whose property the ground was . . . In Bartlett's Passage, which leads from Bartlett's Buildings into Fetter Lane, Charles Lamb was at school before he went to Christ's Hospital " (Wheatley, *London*, i, 121.)

5. **Bedford** [Coffee-house], **The,** (1) where John Thorpe professed to have met General Tilney " for ever." *N.A.*xii. Tom Musgrave " was detained chatting at the Bedford by a friend." *Watsons*, 355. The Bedford stood at the north-east corner of the Piazza, Covent Garden. It was frequented by Foote, Garrick, Quin, Fielding, Hogarth, Sheridan and many other well-known men. " ' This coffee-house,' says *The Connoisseur*, in 1754, ' is every night crowded with men of parts. Almost every one you meet is a polite scholar and a wit.' Later it was the home of the Beef Steak Society, whose laureate in the Sheridan era was Captain Charles Morris of the ' Life Guards ' and the musical ' Toper's Apology.' " (A. Dobson, *Eighteenth-century Vignettes*, 3d. series. " Tour of Covent Garden.")

6. **Bedford Square.** *M.P.*xlv.

7. **Belgrave Chapel** was attended by J.A. in 1813, *Life*, 268.

8. **Berkeley Street,** in which Mrs. Jennings's house was situated. *S.S.*xxvii. Cf. No. 43.

9. **Bond Street.** (1) I met Colonel Brandon Monday morning in Bond Street. *S.S.*xx. (2) Mr. Elton was to leave Emma's drawing of Harriet Smith in Bond Street for framing. *E.*vii. " Bond Street . . . has long stood as the representation of fashionable habits as well as the resort of the fashionable lounger. Bond Street loungers are mentioned in the *Weekly Journal* of June 1, 1717." (Wheatley, *London* i, 221.)

10. **British Gallery,** in Pall Mall, was visited by J.A. in 1811. *Life*, 245. This was the gallery at the British Institution, 52 Pall Mall. " Two exhibitions were held in the course of every year—one of living artists in the winter, and one of old masters in the summer." (Wheatley, *London*, i, 251.)

11. **Brompton,** 16 St. Michael's Place, where the Henry Austens were living when J.A. visited them in 1808—" a row of houses on the site of the present Egerton Mansions." *Life*, 204n.

12. **Brunswick Square,** where lived John and Isabella Knightley. *E.*1.

13. **Camberwell.** A most respectable Girls Boarding School, or Academy, from Camberwell. *Sand.* v.

14. **Carlton House,** where the Rev. J. S. Clarke, the

librarian, instructed by the Prince Regent, showed J.A. the Library and other apartments in 1815. *Life*, 312. Carlton House occupied the present open space between the foot of Regent Street and the steps leading down to the Mall, at the top of which stands the Duke of York column. It was pulled down in 1826, and the columns of the portico were used at the National Gallery in 1835.

15. **Cheapside.** " If they had uncles enough to fill *all* Cheapside," cried Bingley, " it would not make them one jot less agreeable." *P.P.*viii.

16. **Conduit Street,** where the Middletons stayed when in town. *S.S.*xxvii.

17. **Cork Street,** where J.A. was staying in 1796. *Life*, 99 : *Lett.* i, 133.

18. **Covent Garden Theatre,** (1) visited by J. in September, 1813, and March, 1814. *Life*, 274, 295. (2) Philander and Gustavus . . . removed to Covent Garden, where they still exhibited under the assumed names of *Luvis* and *Quick*. *L. & F.* 42. The Theatre visited by J.A. was the house (the third on the site) designed by Smirke, which was built after the fire of 1809, later to be again burned and rebuilt.

19. **Drury Lane Theatre,** (1) where J.A. saw Kean in *Shylock*, in March, 1814. *Life*, 294 : *Mem.* vi. (2) Last night in Drury Lane lobby, I ran against Sir John Middleton. *S.S.*xliv. The Drury Lane visited by J. was the fourth theatre on the site, built 1811–12. That which saw the rencontre

mentioned in (2) was the third, viz., the theatre rebuilt after the destruction in 1741 of the house built by Wren, and opened in 1774, and itself burnt in 1809.

20. **Edward Street,** (1) where Mrs. Younge let lodgings. *P.P.*li ; and (2) where the Johnsons lived. *Lady S.*, Lett. 7. Edward Street, Portland Chapel was destroyed some time before 1828 to make way for Langham Place.

21. **Exeter Exchange** [in the Strand]. John Dashwood took " Harry to see the wild beasts at Exeter Exchange." *S.S.*xxxiii. " The little crowded nest of shop-counters and wild beasts, called Exeter Change, which has lately been pulled down, took its name from a mansion belonging to the Bishop of Exeter . . . Exeter Change was supposed to have been built in the reign of William and Mary, as a speculation." (Leigh Hunt, *The Town*, Ch. iv). The menagerie visited by the Dashwoods was on the upper floor. Exeter Exchange was demolished in 1829, and its site is now occupied by Burleigh Street.

22. **Gracechurch Street,** where the Gardiners lived. *P.P.*xxv.

23. **Gray's,** a jeweller's shop " in Sackville Street, where Elinor was carrying on a negotiation for the exchange of a few old-fashioned jewels of her mother." *S.S.*xxxiii.

24. **Gray's Inn.** Mr. Beard, a solicitor, of Gray's Inn. *Sand.* vi.

25. **Grosvenor Street,** (1) where Mr. Hurst had a house. *P.P.*xxi ; and (2) where Mrs. Marlowe lived. " Les. C." in *L. & F.* 73.

26. **Hanover Square,** where the Palmers lived. *S.S.*xx. Hanover Square was built about 1718. See also No. 47.

27. **Hans Place,** No. 23, where J.A. visited the Henry Austens in 1814 and 1815. *Life,* 305, 309. Hans Place, Sloane Street, was named after Sir Hans Sloane, the famous physician.

28. **Harley Street,** where the John Dashwoods " had taken a very good house for three months." *S.S.*xxxiv.

29. **Henrietta Street,** Covent Garden, No. 10, where the Henry Austens were living, when J.A. visited them in September, 1813, and March, 1814. *Life,* 273, 291. This street was " most fashionably inhabited when first erected—" in 1637. (Wheatley, *London,* ii, 207). Henry Austen in 1813–14 was partner in a bank, whose offices were close by No. 10.

30. **Hill Street,** where Admiral and Mrs. Crawford lived. *M.P.*v.

31. **Holborn.** (1) I think of going as far as Holborn to-day. *S.S.*xl. (2) " Holbourn." *L. & F.* 19. *See also* No. 4.

32. **Kensington Gardens,** (1) in which J.A. had " a pleasant walk " in 1811. *Lett.* ii, 94. (2) The third day . . . was so fine, so beautiful a Sunday, as to draw many to Kensington Gardens. *S.S.* xxxviii.

33. **Keppel Street,** where J. made a call in 1815. *Lett.* ii, 255.

34. **Limehouse,** Captain Little, of, a Library subscriber at Sanditon. *Sand.* vi.

35. **Little Theatre, The.** *P.P.*li. It stood on the north of the present Haymarket Theatre site, and was pulled down in 1821.

36. **Liverpool Museum,** perhaps Bullock's Natural History Museum, 22 Piccadilly. It was visited by J.A. in 1811. *Life*, 245.

37. **Lyceum Theatre,** visited by J.A. in 1811 and 1813. *Life*, 249, 279. The Lyceum Theatre, built in 1765, was at first used for exhibitions and concerts. It was turned into a theatre in 1790 ; was altered in 1809 into the " English Opera House " ; and was burned down in 1830. The present building, on the same site, was opened in 1834. (Wheatley, *London*, ii, 451, 452.)

38. **Manchester Street,** where the Enscombe family, the Churchills, stayed when in town. *E.*xxxvii.

39. **Merchant Taylors'** [School]. John was at Oxford, Edward at Merchant Taylors'. *N.A.*iv. This School was founded, in Suffolk Lane, in 1561. A new School was built in 1675, and was several times enlarged, especially in 1829. This was pulled down, and new buildings were erected on the site vacated by the Charterhouse Schools. The new School was opened in 1875.

40. **Newgate Prison.** *L. & F.* 20.

41. **Pall Mall.** (1) A stationer's shop in Pall Mall, where I had business. *S.S.*xxx. (2) Edward [Ferrars] . . . is lodging at No — Pall Mall. *S.S.* xxxviii. *See also* No. 10.

42. **Park Street,** [Grosvenor Square] where Mrs. Ferrars lived. *S.S.*xxii.

43. **Portman Square.** (1) Mrs. Jennings " resided every winter in a house in one of the streets near Portman Square " [Cf. No. 8, **Berkeley Street.**] *S.S.*xxv. (2) Miss Margaret Lesley writes to her dear Charlotte Lutterell from Portman Square. " Les. C." in *L. & F.* 76.

44. **Sackville Street.** (1) Gray's, the jewellers, in Sackville Street. *S.S.*xxxiii. (2) " C. of L." in *L. & F.* 117.

45. **St. Clement's Church,** where Wickham and Lydia Bennet were married. *P.P.*li.

46. **St. George's Fields.** *N.A.*xiv.

47. **St. George's, Hanover Square.** Perhaps you would not mind passing through London, and seeing the inside of St. George's, Hanover Square. *M.P.*xliii.

48. **St. James's Street,** where Colonel Brandon lodged. *S.S.*xl.

49. **St. Paul's.** My dear child, commend Dr. Grant to the deanery of . . . St. Paul's. *M.P.*xxii.

50. **Sloane Street,** No. 64, where the Henry Austens lived when visited by J. in 1811 and 1813. *Life,* 244, 265.

G

51. **Spring Gardens,** Picture Exhibition at, in 1813. *Life*, 267. " 'The Great Room in Spring Gardens,' where the Society of Artists held their exhibitions for several years." (Wheatley, *London*, iii, 297.)

52. **Tattersal's.** They must have been seen together ... at Tattersal's. *Pers.* i. Tattersall's, Grosvenor Place, was so called after Richard Tattersall, who died in 1795. It " was entered by a narrow lane, at the side of St. George's Hospital." (Wheatley, *London*, iii, 347). The building was demolished in 1866.

53. **Temple, The.** (1) Young men who had chambers in the Temple. *S.S.*xix. (2) Mr. Elliot had chambers in the Temple. *Pers.* xxi.

54. **Tower, The.** *N.A.*xiv.

55. **Upper Seymour Street.** I can get you however a very nice Drawingroom-apartment in Upper Seymour Street. *Lady S.*, Lett. 26.

56. **Vauxhall.** I always longed particularly to go to Vauxhall, to see whether the cold Beef there is cut so thin as it is reported. " Les. C." in *L. & F.* 68. It was ham that was reputed to be cut with such astonishing thinness at Vauxhall. " It was rumoured, too . . . that there, carvers were exercised in the mystic art of cutting a moderate-sized ham into slices thin enough to pave the whole of the grounds," [about eleven acres.] Dickens, " Vauxhall Gardens by Day," in *Sketches by Boz*, " Scenes," xiv. There is an excellent account of " Old Vaux-

hall Gardens," with all their literary associations, in Austin Dobson's *Eighteenth-century Vignettes*, 1st Series.

57. **Westminster** [School]. (1) If you had only sent him to Westminster as well as myself . . . all this would have been prevented. *S.S.*xxxvi. (2) My plan was laid at Westminster, a little altered, perhaps, at Cambridge. *M.P.*vi.

58. **Wigmore Street**, No. 10. *Lady S.*, Lett. 2.

59. **Wimpole Street,** where Mrs. Rushworth had " one of the best houses." *M.P.*xl.

Long, Mrs., an acquaintance of Mrs. Bennet. *P.P.*i.

Longbourn, Hertfordshire, the village where the Bennets lived. *P.P.*iii.

Longstaple, near Plymouth, where Mr. Pratt lived. *S.S.*xxii.

Longtown, The Marquis of. Being disappointed in my hope of seeing the Marquis of Longtown. *N.A.*xvii.

" Love and Freindship," a volume of early stories and sketches by J.A. The book was first printed from the original MSS. and published by Messrs. Chatto and Windus in 1922, with a preface by G. K. Chesterton. The small volume contained " Love and Freindship "; " Lesley Castle " ; " The History of England " ; " A Collection of Letters " ; and " Scraps." In his preface Mr. Chesterton says—" She is said to have written these things at the age of seventeen." But the end of *Love and Freindship* is dated June 13, 1790, when the author was but fourteen and a half years old, which makes that spirited little essay in irony and burlesque a remarkable example of precocity.

Lovelace [Richardson's]. We felt that he was formed to be a dangerous Man—quite in the line of the Lovelaces. *Sand.* viii.

" Lovers' Vows," the play. *M.P.*xiii. There were several English versions of Kotzebue's *Natural Son* published under the title of *Lovers' Vows.* The most popular was that by Mrs. Inchbald, first produced at Covent Garden in October, 1798, and this was the version proposed to be acted at Mansfield Park.

Lower Rooms. *See* **Bath.**

Lucas, Sir William, Knight. *P.P.*i, vi. Sir William Lucas had been formerly in trade in Meryton, where he had made a tolerable fortune, and risen to the honour of knighthood by an address to the king during his Mayoralty. v.

Lucas, Lady. *P.P.*i, xviii. Lady Lucas was a very good kind of woman, not too clever to be a valuable neighbour to Mrs. Bennet. *P.P.*v.

Lucas, Charlotte, their eldest child. *P.P.*iii. A sensible, intelligent young woman, about twenty-seven, was Elizabeth's intimate friend. *P.P.*v.

Lucas, Maria, their second daughter. *P.P.*iii. A good humoured girl, but as empty-headed as himself [Sir William]. *P.P.*xxvii.

Lucas, " A young," brother to Charlotte and Maria. If I were as rich as Mr. Darcy [the boy cried] . . . I should not care how proud I was. I would keep a pack of fox hounds, and drink a bottle of wine every day. *P.P.*v.

Lucas Lodge, the residence of the Lucas family. *P.P.*v.

Lutterell, Charlotte. "Les. C." in *L. & F.* 47.

Lutterell, Eloisa, her sister. *Ibid.* 51.

Luvis, the stage name of Philander. *L. & F.* 42.

Lyceum Theatre. *See* **London.**

Lyford, Mr., the Basingstoke doctor who attended J.A.'s mother. *Life,* 115. The Mr. Lyford who attended J. during her last illness, at Winchester (*Life,* 388) was presumably the same medical man.

Lyme Regis, Dorset. (1) J.A. and her parents spent some weeks at Lyme in the autumn of 1804. *Life,* 176. (2) Lyme was where Captain Harville and his family had settled for the winter. *Pers.* xi ; and where Louisa Musgrove fell from the Cobb. *Ibid.* xii.

Lyncombe, near Bath, to which J. walked. *Life,* 169.

M

Macartney, Lord. How does Lord Macartney go on ? —(opening a volume on the table). *M.P.*xvi. Lord Macartney's *Journal of the Embassy to China* was published in Sir John Barrow's *Some Account of the Public Life, and a Selection from the Unpublished Writings of the Earl of Macartney,* in 1807.

"Macbeth." (1) *M.P.*xiv. (2) One of our most admiral Performances was *Macbeth*, in which we were truly great. *L. & F.* 41.

Macbeths, The, the Macduffs, the M'Leods, the M'Kenzies, the M'Phersons, the M'Cartneys, the M'Donalds, the M'kinnons, the M'lellams, the M'kays. We visit no one but the M'Leods, etc. "Les. C." in *L. & F.* 48.

Macdonald, —, Sophia's cousin. The Door of the Apartment opened and "Macdonald" was announced. *L. & F.* 23.

Macdonald-Hall, his residence. *L. & F.* 24.

Macdonald, Janetta, his daughter. *L. & F.* 24.

M'Kenrie, Captain. She said that she believed she *did like* Captain M'Kenrie better than any one she knew besides. *L. & F.* 25.

Mackenzie, Sir Walter Elliot's gardener at Kellynch House. I have been several times in the gardens with Mackenzie, trying to understand, and make him understand, which of Elizabeth's plants are for Lady Russell. *Pers.* v.

Maclean, Lady Mary. Old Lady Mary Maclean? I need not ask after her. *Pers.* xxi...

Maddison, Henry Crawford's agent at Everingham. I am not satisfied about Maddison. I am sure he still means to impose on me if possible. *M.P.*xlii.

Maddox, Charles. Charles Maddox is as gentlemanlike a man as you will see anywhere. *M.P.*xv.

Maddoxes, The Miss. She could not recollect what it was that she had heard about one of the Miss Maddoxes *M.P.*xxix.

Magdalen Bridge, Oxford. I chanced to meet him on Magdalen Bridge, as he was driving into Oxford last term. *N.A.*vii.

Maid, Miss Tilney's. This ill-time intruder was Miss Tilney's maid. *N.A.*xxi. Perhaps she was the " Alice " of Ch. xxviii.

Manchester Street. *See* **London.**

" Mansfield Park " was begun in 1811 and completed "soon after June, 1813." *Life*, 290. It was being read by the author's brother Henry, as they travelled together to London, in March, 1814, and was published in May of that year by T. Egerton, of the Military Library, Whitehall. It was issued in three volumes, in boards, at 18/-. The small first edition was exhausted in less than six months. The second edition was not published till 1816, when John Murray brought it out.

Mansfield, the parish in which Mansfield Park was situated. *M.P.*i.

Mansfield Common. She has a great desire to get as far as Mansfield Common. *M.P.*vii.

Mansfield Park, in the county of Northampton, Sir Thomas Bertram's seat. *M.P.*i.

Mansfield Parsonage, the home at first of Mr. and Mrs. Norris, later of Dr. and Mrs. Grant. *M.P.*i.

Mansfield Wood. The first day I went over Mansfield Wood, and Edmund took the copses beyond Easton, and we brought home six brace between us. *M.P.*xix.

Manwaring, Mr. Manwaring is so uncommonly pleasing ... I remember saying to myself ... " I like this man ; pray Heaven no harm come of it ! " *Lady S.*, Lett. 2.

Manwaring, Mrs. [is] insupportably jealous. *Ibid.*, Lett. 2.

Manwaring, Maria, their daughter. Sir James Martin, on whom I bestowed a little notice in order to detach him from Miss Manwaring. *Ibid.*, Lett. 2.

Manydown Park—" a substantial old manor-house . . . which stands between Steventon and Basingstoke." (*Life*, 68). It was the home of Mr. Bigg Wither and his daughters, the Miss Biggs (*q.v.*)—who " kept the name Bigg, though father and brother became Bigg Wither." (*Life*, 68n.)   It is often mentioned in the *Letters.*

Maple Grove. My   brother   Mr.   Suckling's   seat. *E.*xxxii.

Mapleton, Dr., and family, friends of J.A. at Bath, 1799. *Life*, 129 ; *Lett.* i, 221, 222.

Mapleton, Marianne, *d.* May, 1801. Many a girl on early death has been praised into an angel, I believe, on slighter pretensions to beauty, sense, and merit, than Marianne.   J.A. to C. *Life*, 169 ; *Lett.* i, 293

Margaret, sister to Augusta. Poor Augusta could scarcely breathe, while Margaret was all Life and Rapture.   " C. of L." in *L. & F.* 104.

Margaret of Anjou. A woman whose distresses and misfortunes were so great as almost to make me, who hate her, pity her. "H. of E." in *L. & F.* 86.

Maria, a character in the "First Act of a Comedy." "Scraps" in *L. & F.* 133.

Marianne, daughter of Isabel, one of the correspondents in *Love and Freindship. L. & F.* 6.

Marina. "Scraps" in *L. & F.* 140.

Market Place. *See* **Bath.**

Marlborough. The only ten minutes I have spent out of my chaise since that time procured me a nuncheon at Marlborough. *S.S.*xliv.

Marlborough Buildings. *See* **Bath.**

Marlowe, Mr. and Mrs. [Emma] are very agreeable people. "Les. C." in *L. & F.* 59.

"Marmion." Trying to ascertain whether *Marmion* or *The Lady of the Lake* were to be preferred. *Pers.* xi.

Marshall, Captain, William Price's captain. *M.P.*vi.

Marshall, Mr. Mr. Marshall and Mr. Hemming change their dress every day of their lives before dinner. *Watsons,* 351.

Martin. A family of the name of Martin. *E.*iii.

Martin, Colonel, "of the Horse Guards." "Scraps" in *L. & F.* 136.

Martin, Elizabeth, sister of Robert, and another sister unnamed. I shall always have a great regard for the Miss Martins, especially Elizabeth. *E.*iv, xxi.

Martin, Mrs., mother of Robert and Elizabeth, who had " *two* parlours, two very good parlours, indeed." *E*.iv.

Martin, Robert, a farmer in the parish of Donwell. Harriet . . . dwelt a good deal upon his being so very good-humoured and obliging. . . . She believed he was very clever, and understood everything . . . not handsome—not at all handsome. I thought him very plain at first, but I do not think him so plain now. *E*.iv.

Martin, Sir James. *Lady S.*, Lett. 2.

Martin, Sir John, " who died immensely rich." " Scraps " in *L. & F.* 136.

Martin, Sir Thomas, son of Sir John. *Ibid.* 136.

Mary, maid at Mrs. Smith's lodgings. If you will have the goodness to ring for Mary. *Pers.* xxi.

Mary, maid in Laura's family. I think I hear Mary going to the door. *L. & F.* 9.

Mary, daughter of Henry VII. The youngest [daughter] Mary, married first the King of France, and secondly the Duke of Suffolk. " H. of E." in *L. & F.* 88.

Mary [Queen], daughter of Henry VIII. *Ibid.* 91.

Mason, Miss. " C. of L." in *L. & F.* 112.

Mathew, Anne, *m.* James Austen (*q.v.*)

Mathews, Mrs., Miss., Miss E., Miss H., all visitors at Sanditon. *Sand.* vi.

Matilda, friend of Henrietta Halton. There is a pattern for a Love-letter, Matilda ! " C. of L." in *L. & F.* 118.

Matilda, *See* **St. Clair.**

Matlock. The celebrated beauties of Matlock, Chatsworth . . . *P.P.*xlii.

Maxwell, Mrs. Admiral, godmother of little Mary Price. It was the gift of her good godmother, old Mrs. Admiral Maxwell. *M.P.*xxxviii.

Mediterranean, The. (1) A small sketch of a ship sent four years ago from the Mediterranean by William. *M.P.*xvi. (2) I had still the same luck in the Mediterranean. *Pers.* viii.

Merchant-Taylors'. *See* **London.**

Merryweather, Miss, a visitor at Sanditon. *Sand.* vi.

Meryton, Herts., a country town near the residences of the Bennets, Lucases and Bingleys. *P.P.*iv.

Metcalfe, Lady. Lady Metcalfe . . . finds Miss Pope a treasure. *P.P.*xxix.

Mickleham, Surrey. Let my accents swell to Mickleham on one side, and Dorking on the other. *E.*xliii.

Middlesex. My Father's house is situated in Bedfordshire, my Aunt's in Middlesex. *L. & F.* 10.

Middleton, Sir John. *S.S.*iv. A good-looking man, about forty. *S.S.*vi.

Middleton, Mary, Lady. *S.S.*v. Her face was handsome, her figure tall and striking, and her address graceful . . . though perfectly well bred, she was reserved, cold, and had nothing to say for herself beyond the most commonplace inquiry or remark. *S.S.*vi.

Middleton, John, their eldest child, a fine little boy about six years old. *S.S.*vi. The name appears in Ch. xxi.

Middleton, William, the second child. How playful William is ! *S.S.*xxi.

Middleton, Anna Maria, the three-year-old daughter. " And here is my sweet little Anna-Maria ? . . . who had not made a noise for the last two minutes." *S.S.*xxi.

" Midnight Bell." *N.A.*vi. By F. Lathom, published in 1798.

Millar, Colonel. I cried for two days together when Colonel Millar's regiment went away. *P.P.*xli.

Millar, Mr. " Scraps " in *L. & F.* 131.

Millar, Charlotte and Julia, his daughters. They are certainly extremely pretty. *Ibid.* 131.

Milmans, The two. *E.*xxxii. *See* **Bird** and **Cooper.**

Milsom Street. *See* **Bath.**

Milton. Some dozen lines of Milton, Pope, and Prior. *N.A.*v.

Minehead, Somerset. *Pers.* xviii.

Mirror, The, a periodical paper. There is a very clever essay in one of the books upstairs . . . *The Mirror,* I think. *N.A.*xxx. *The Mirror* was edited by Henry Mackenzie, and ran from January 23, 1779, to May 27, 1780. The essay referred to is in No. 63.

Mitchell, Farmer. He darted away with so much gallantry and borrowed two umbrellas for us from Farmer Mitchell's. *E.*i.

Mitchell, Anne. Anne Mitchell had tried to put on a turban like mine . . . but made wretched work of it. *N.A.*xxvii.

Mitchells, The. I daresay it will not be a very good ball. I know the Mitchells will not be there. *N.A.*xi.

Molland's. *See* **Bath.**

"Monk," The. There has not been a tolerably decent one [novel] come out since *Tom Jones*, except *The Monk N.A.*vii. This once famous novel, by M. G. Lewis, was published in 1796.

Monkford, Somerset. I remember no gentleman resident at Monkford since the time of old Governor Trent. *Pers.* iii.

Montgomery, the poet. Montgomery has all the Fire of Poetry. *Sand.* vii.

Moon, The, an inn room. "Scraps" in *L. & F.* 133.

Morgan, man-servant to the Parkers. Here is something at hand, pleasanter still—Morgan, with his "Dinner on Table." *Sand.* v.

Morland, Catherine. No one who had ever seen Catherine Morland in her infancy would have supposed her born to be a heroine. *N.A.*i.

Morland, George and Harriet, a brother and sister. *N.A.*xxix.

Morland, James, Catherine's eldest brother—"of a very amiable disposition, and sincerely attached to her." *N.A.*iv, vii.

Morland, Mrs., the mother of the family. Her mother

was a woman of useful, plain sense, with a good temper, and, what is more remarkable, with a good constitution. *N.A.*i.

Morland, Richard, the father. Her father was a clergyman, without being neglected, or poor, and a very respectable man, though his name was Richard— and he had never been handsome. *N.A.*i.

Morland, Sarah or **Sally,** Catherine's sister. *N.A.*i, xxix.

Morley, Sir Basil. A friend of mine who was standing near (Sir Basil Morley). *Pers.* iii.

Morning Post, The. These advertisements which I cut out myself from the Morning Post and the Kentish Gazette. *Sand.* i.

Morris, Mr., who let Netherfield Park to Mr. Bingley. *P.P.*i.

Morton, The Hon. Miss, " only daughter of the late Lord Morton, with thirty thousand pounds." *S.S.*xxxiii.

Morton, The late Lord. *S.S.*xxxiii.

Moss, Rev. T., author of *Poems on Several Occasions*, 1769, in which the first is the " Beggar's Petition," mentioned in *N.A.*i.

Motherbank, The, Portsmouth. He talked only of the dockyard, the harbour, Spithead, and the Mother-bank. *M.P.*xxxix.

Mounteagle, Lord. " H. of E." in *L. & F.* 94.

Moyes, J., Greville Street, Hatton Garden, London, printer of Vol. III. of the first edition of *Emma*, 1816.

Mullinses, The. I think you had better mention the poor Mullins's situation and sound her Ladyship as to a Subscription for them. *Sand.* xii.

Murray, John, Albemarle Street, London, publisher of the first editions of *Emma* 3 vols. 1816 ; *Northanger Abbey* and *Persuasion*, 4 vols., 1818 ; and of the second edition of *Mansfield Park*, 1816. J.A. had some correspondence with him in 1815. (*Lett.* ii, 249.)

Musgrave, Mrs., a connection of Cassandra Austen (1) (*q.v.*), was one of J.A.'s godparents.

Musgrave, Tom, who " generally pays attention to every new girl, but he is a great flirt and never means anything serious." *Watsons,* 298, 315.

Musgrove, Mr. and Mrs., of Uppercross Great House. Mr. and Mrs. Musgrove were a very good sort of people ; friendly and hospitable, not much educated, and not at all elegant. *Pers.* v, vi.

Musgrove, Charles, (1) their eldest son, of Uppercross Cottage. *Pers.* i. Charles Musgrove was civil and agreeable ; in sense and temper he was undoubtedly superior to his wife. *Ibid.* vi.

Musgrove, Mary, his wife, *née* Elliot. *Pers.* i. Mary, often a little unwell, and always thinking a great deal of her own complaints. *Ibid.* v.

Musgrove, Charles (2) **and Walter,** small sons of Charles and Mary. Little Charles does not mind a word I say, and Walter is growing quite as bad. *Ibid.* v, vi.

Musgrove, Henrietta and Louisa, sisters of Charles Musgrove (1). Young ladies of nineteen and twenty, who had brought from a school at Exeter all the usual stock of accomplishments, and were now . . . living to be fashionable, happy, and merry. *Pers.* v, vi.

Musgrove, Richard, brother of Charles, Henrietta and Louisa, died abroad at the age of nineteen. A very troublesome, hopeless son. *Ibid.* vi.

Musgrove, Thomas. " C. of L." in *L. & F.* 117. A Musgrove is not to be met with by every girl. *Ibid.* 119.

" My Grandmother " [by Prince Hoare], An allusion to. *M.P.*xiii.

"Mysterious Warnings." *N.A.*vi. This was *The Mysterious Warning*, by Mrs. Parsons, published in 1796.

"Mystery, The," a childish fragment of comedy, by J.A. *Mem.* iii.

N

Nackington, near Rowling (*q.v.*) J.A. dined there in September, 1796. *Lett.* ii, 141.

Nanny, the cook at Steventon. *Life,* 112.

Nanny, Mrs. Norris's maid. I will send Nanny to London on purpose. *M.P.*i.

Nanny, the Watsons' maid. First of all Nanny shall bring in the dinner. *Watsons,* 334.

Naples. We have the pleasure of finding that he is at Naples. " Les. C." in *L. & F.* 78.

Nash, Miss, one of Mrs. Goddard's three teachers. *E*.iv.

"Necromancer of the Black Forest." *N.A.*vi. This was by P. Teuthold, and was published in 1794.

Netherfield Park, rented by Mr. Bingley. *P.P.*i.

Neville. I am not conscious of being more sincerely attached to Willoughby than I was to Neville. "C. of L." in *L. & F.* 105.

Newbury, Berkshire. They . . . made no stop anywhere till they reached Newbury, where a comfortable meal . . . wound up the enjoyments and fatigues of the day. *M.P.*xxxviii.

Newcastle-on-Tyne. We shall be at Newcastle all the winter. *P.P.*li.

Newgate. *See* **London.**

New London Inn, Exeter. I see Mr. Ferrars myself, ma'am, this morning in Exeter, and his lady too . . . they was stopping in a chaise at the door of the New London Inn. *S.S.*xlvii.

Newmarket. Tom had gone . . . with a party of young men to Newmarket. *M.P.*xliv.

Newton, Devonshire. Here are the two Miss Careys come over from Newton. *S.S.*xiii.

Nicholls, Mrs., housekeeper at Netherfield. As soon as Nicholls has made white soup enough I shall send round my cards. *P.P.*xi.

Norfolk. (1) She would settle on him the Norfolk estate, which, clear of land-tax, brings in a good

H

thousand a year. *S.S.*xxxvii. (2) The son had a good estate in Norfolk. *M.P.*iv.

Norfolk, The Duke of. His Majesty's fifth Wife was the Duke of Norfolk's Niece. " H. of E." in *L. & F.* 89.

Norland Common. The enclosure of Norland Common, now carrying on, is a most serious drain. *S.S.*xxxiii.

Norland Park, Sussex. The seat of the Dashwoods. Their residence was at Norland Park. *S.S.*i.

Norris, Mr., Rector of Mansfield. Poor Mr. Norris's indifferent state of health . . . he could no more bear the noise of a child than he could fly. *M.P.*i.

Norris, Mrs., *née* Ward, his wife. Had there been a family to provide for, Mrs. Norris might never have saved her money ; but having no care of that kind, there was nothing to impede her frugality. *M.P.*i.

Northam, near Southampton, to which J. made an excursion in 1808. *Life,* 218.

Northampton. (1) The little girl . . . at Northampton was met by Mrs. Norris. *M.P.*ii. (2) The 12th Light Dragoons . . . called up from Northampton to quell the insurgents. *N.A.*xiv.

Northamptonshire, the county of Mansfield Park. *M.P.*i.

" Northanger Abbey," " though not prepared for the press till 1803, was certainly first composed in 1798." (*Mem.* iii.) *Northanger Abbey* (probably called *Susan*), was written in 1797 and 1798. (*Life,* 96.) It was sold to Messrs. Crosby & Son, of London, in 1803 for £10 (*Life*, 174) and was recovered by the author for the same amount about 1815. (*See* **Crosby.**)

The novel was published posthumously (with *Persuasion*) by John Murray, in four volumes, in 1818, at the price of 24s.   A "Biographical Notice of the Author," by her brother Henry, was prefixed.

Northanger Abbey, Gloucestershire, the home of the Tilneys.   *N.A.* xvii.

North Seas.   The winter that I passed by myself at Deal, when the Admiral (*Captain* Croft then) was in the North Seas.   *Pers.* viii.

Northumberland, The Duke of.   " H. of E." in *L. & F.* 90.

North Yarmouth.   Sitting down together in our lodgings at North Yarmouth.   *Pers.* x.

Norton, Mr.   Mr. Norton is a cousin of Captain Hunter's.   *Watsons*, 328.

Norval, in Home's *Douglas*.   I am sure *my name was Norval* every evening of my life through our Christmas holidays.   *M.P.*xiii.

Noyce, Fanny.   The particular friend of *my* very particular friend Fanny Noyce.   *Sand.* ix.

O

Oakham Mount, near Longbourn.   I advise Mr. Darcy, and Lizzy and Kitty . . . to walk to Oakham Mount this morning . . . Mr. Darcy has never seen the view.   *P.P.*lix.

Oakley and **Oakley Hall.** On Thursday we walked [from Steventon] to Deane, yesterday to Oakley Hall and Oakley. *Lett.* i, 231.

O'Brien, Captain. It did not suit Captain O'Brien that I should be one of the party. *Watsons*, 313.

O'Brien, Mrs., his wife, formerly Mrs. Turner, aunt to the Watson girls. *Watsons*, 313.

Old Bridge. *See* **Bath.**

Oliver, Tom. Tom Oliver is a very clever fellow. *M.P.* xv.

Oriel College, Oxford. Jackson of Oriel, bid me sixty at once. *N.A.* vii.

Ormond, The Duke of. "H. of E." in *L. & F.*, 96.

" Orphan of the Rhine." *N.A.* vi. This was by Eleanor Steath, and was published in 1798.

Osborne, Lady. Lady Osborne had by much the finest person ; though nearly fifty, she was very handsome, and had all the dignity of rank. *Watsons*, 317.

Osborne, Lord, her son. Lord Osborne was a very fine young man ; but there was an air of coldness, of carelessness, even of awkwardness about him. *Watsons*, 315, 317.

Osborne, Miss, her daughter. He will never marry unless he can marry somebody very great ; Miss Osborne, perhaps, or somebody in that style. *Watsons* 303, 317.

Osborne Castle, the residence of the Osborne family.

Two carriages are ordered from the White Hart to be at Osborne Castle by nine. *Watsons*, 309.

Osbornes, The. Sanguine hopes were entertained that the Osbornes themselves would be there. *Watsons*, 297.

Ostalis, La Comtesse d', in Madame de Genlis' *Adelaide and Theodore*. She has had the advantage, you know, of practising on me . . . like La Baronne d'Almane on La Comtesse d'Ostalis. *E*.liii.

"Othello." Neither Hamlet nor . . Othello . . . presented anything that could satisfy even the tragedians. *M.P.*xiv.

Otway, Mr., Mrs., Miss, Miss Caroline, Mr. George, Mr. Arthur, are all mentioned by Miss Bates as among the friends she was meeting at the ball at the Crown Inn, Highbury. *E*.xxxviii.

Owen, Mr., a friend of Edmund Bertram. *M.P.*xxix.

Owen, The Misses. His friend Mr. Owen had sisters —he might find them attractive . . . "How many Miss Owens are there ? " " Three grown up." *M.P.*xxix.

Oxford. (1) J.A., in very early life, spent a short time at Oxford, with her sister, under the care of Mrs. Cawley (*q.v.*) (2) I was therefore entered at Oxford, and have been properly idle ever since. *S.S.*xix. (3) *P.P.*xlii. (4) His leaving Eton for Oxford made no change in his kind dispositions. *M.P.*ii. (5) Frank . . . is at Oxford to-day. *E*.xxiii. (6) John was at Oxford. *N.A.*iv. (7) The inhabitants of Oxford who were always loyal to their King. " H. of E." in *L. & F.* 95.

P

Pall Mall. *See* **London.**

Palmer, Fanny, of Bermuda, the first wife of Charles Austen (*q.v.*)

Palmer, Harriet, her sister, the second wife of Charles Austen.

Palmer, Thomas. A grave-looking young man of five or six-and-twenty, with an air of more fashion and sense than his wife, but of less willingness to please, or be pleased. *S.S.*xix.

Palmer, Charlotte, his wife, daughter of Mrs. Jennings, and sister of Lady Middleton. Mrs. Palmer . . . was short and plump, had a very pretty face, and the finest expression of good humour in it that could possibly be. *S.S.*xix.

Pangloss, Dr., a character in Colman's *Heir at Law.* Doubting only whether to prefer Lord Duberley or Dr. Pangloss for himself. *M.P.*xiv.

Paragon Buildings. *See* **Bath.**

Paris. My Brother is already in Paris. " Les. C." in *L. & F.* 54.

Parker, Anne. I murdered my father . . . I have since murdered my Mother, and I am now going to murder my Sister. " Scraps " in *L. & F.* 137.

Parker, Arthur, youngest brother of Thomas . . . " is so delicate that he can engage in no Profession." *Sand.* v, x.

Parker, Diana and Susan, sisters of Thomas.   They have wretched health . . . and are subject to a variety of very serious Disorders.   *Sand.* v, ix, x.

Parker, Mary, wife of Thomas.   *Sand.* i.

Parker, Mary, one of their daughters.   You can get a Parasol at Whitby's for little Mary at any time.   *Sand.* iv.

Parker, Sidney, brother of Thomas.   Sidney says anything you know.   *Sand.* iv, xii.

Parker, Thomas, of Sanditon.   *Sand.* i.

Parklands, the home of the De Courcys.   *Lady S.*, Lett. 12.

Park Street.   *See* **London.**

Parry, George.   *N.A.*ii.

Parrys, The.   The Parrys . . . luckily are coming to-night.   *S.S.*xxx.

Parrys, The.   If the Parrys had come . . . she might have danced with George Parry.   *N.A.*ii.

Parsons, Mrs.   *See* **Castle of Wolfenbach** and **Mysterious Warnings.**

Partridge, Clara.   *See* **Jeffereys.**

Partridge, Mrs.—the lady I [Mrs. Elton] have always resided with when in Bath.   *E.*xxxii.

Patty, the Bates's maid.   I was only gone down to speak to Patty again about the pork.   *E.*xxi.

Peak, The, Derbyshire.   The celebrated beauties of Matlock . . . or the Peak.   *P.P.*xlii.

Pemberley House, Darcy's place in Derbyshire, first

mentioned. *P.P.*vi.   A large, handsome stone building, standing well on rising ground, and backed by a ridge of high, woody hills.   *P.P.*xliii.

Pemberley Woods.   Elizabeth . . . watched for the first appearance of Pemberley Woods with some perturbation.   *P.P.*xliii.

Pembrokeshire.   " Scraps " in *L. & F.* 139.

Percy, Sir Henry.   Sir Henry Percy, tho' certainly the best bred man of the party . . . " H. of E." in *L. & F.* 94.

Perrot.   James Leigh, of Scarlets, in Wargrave parish, was the son of Thomas Leigh (*q.v.*) and the only brother of J.A.'s mother.   " The name of Perrot, together with a small estate at Northleigh, in Oxfordshire, had been bequeathed to him by a great uncle " (*Mem.* iv), and he became James Leigh Perrot.   He married Jane Cholmeley, a niece of Sir Montague Cholmeley.   They were childless.   James Leigh Perrot was " a man of considerable natural power, with much of the wit of his uncle, [Theophilus Leigh, *q.v.*], the Master of Balliol " (*Mem.* iv.)   He suffered from gout, and with his wife made frequent visits to Bath, where J.A. several times visited them. (*Life*, 127.)   It was at Bath that Mrs. Perrot was falsely accused of larceny. (*Life*, 131, et seq.)   She died in 1836, her husband in 1817.

Perry, Mr., apothecary at Highbury.   Mr. Perry was an intelligent, gentlemanlike man, whose frequent visits were one of the comforts of Mr. Woodhouse's life. *E.*ii, viii.

Perry, Mrs., his wife. Mrs. Perry drank tea with Mrs. and Miss Bates. *E*.ii.

Perrys, the little. There was a strange rumour in Highbury of all the little Perrys being seen with a slice of Mrs. Weston's wedding-cake in their hands ; but Mr. Woodhouse would never believe it. *E*.ii.

"Persuasion." *Persuasion* was begun in 1815 and finished in July 1816. The last chapter but one was almost immediately re-written and replaced by two chapters (xxii and xxiii), greatly to the improvement of the conclusion of the novel. It was first published posthumously, with *Northanger Abbey*, in four volumes by John Murray, in 1818, at the price of 24s.

Perth. Our old and Mouldering Castle, which is situated two miles from Perth on a bold projecting Rock. " Les. C." in *L. & F.* 48.

Perthshire. I live in Perthshire, you in Sussex. *Ibid.* 49.

Peterborough. He was going to a friend near Peterborough. *M.P.*xxvi.

Petty France, on the way from Bath to Northanger Abbey. The tediousness of a two hours' bait at Petty France, in which there was nothing to be done but to eat without being hungry. *N.A.*xx.

Philander, a grandson of Lord St. Clair (*q.v.*) *L. & F.* 22.

Philip, King of Spain. She married Philip King of Spain who in her sister's reign was famous for building Armadas. " H. of E." in *L. & F.* 91.

Philippa, aunt to Edward Lindsay. Philippa received

us both with every expression of affectionate Love. *L. & F.* 11.

Philippa's husband—not named. *Ibid.* 38.

Philips, Mr., an attorney, who married a sister of Mrs. Bennet. *P.P.*vii.

Philips, Mrs., his wife, *née* Gardiner. *P.P.*vii. Mrs. Philips was always glad to see her nieces. *P.P.*xv.

Philippses, The Miss. " C. of L." in *L. & F.* 103.

Pinny, near Lyme Regis, " with its green chasms between romantic rocks." *Pers.* xi.

Pistolletta, a character in the " First Act of a Comedy." " Scraps " in *L. & F.* 133.

" Pleasures of Hope, The," Campbell in his pleasures of Hope has touched the extreme of our Sensations. *Sand.* vii.

Plymouth and **Plymouth Sound.** (1) He had been staying with some friends near Plymouth. *S.S.*xvi. (2) I brought her into Plymouth ; and . . . we had not been six hours in the Sound, when a gale came on. *Pers.* viii.

Polydore, Laura's father. Your Virtues, my amiable Polydore (addressing himself to my father) . . *L. & F.* 10.

Pomfret Castle. Having prevailed on . . . Richard the 2nd . . . to retire for the rest of his life to Pomfret Castle, where he happened to be murdered. " H. of E." in *L. & F.* 85.

Pope, the poet. (1) You have received every assurance

of his admiring Pope no more than is proper. *S.S.*x.
(2) Do you remember Hawkins Browne's " Address
to Tobacco," in imitation of Pope ? *M.P.*xvii.
(3) Pope quoted. *N.A.*i.

Pope, Miss, a governess patronized by Lady C. de Bourgh.
*P.P.*xxix.

Pope, The. He . . . obtained one of the Pope's Bulls
for annulling his 1st Marriage. " Les. C." in *L. & F.*
79.

Popgun, a character in " The First Act of a Comedy."
" Scraps " in *L. & F.* 133.

Portman Square. *See* **London.**

Portsmouth. (1) They may easily get her from Portsmouth to town by the coach. *M.P.*i. (2) You your-
self brought . . . round from Portsmouth to Plymouth.
Pers. viii.

Powlett, C., who wanted to give J.A. a kiss—see her
letter of January 14, 1796. *Life,* 99.

Pratt, Mr., the Miss Steeles' uncle. *S.S.*xxii.

Pratt, Mr., an officer at Meryton. Denny, and Wickham,
and Pratt, and two or three more of the men came
in. *P.P.*xxxix.

Pratt, Mr. Richard, a visitor at Sanditon. *Sand.* vi.

Prescott, Lady. She could not recollect . . . what it
was that Lady Prescott had noticed in Fanny. *M.P.*
xxix.

Price, Betsey, sister of Fanny. *M.P.*xxxvii. The
youngest of the family, about five. *M.P.*xxxviii.

Price, Fanny, eldest daughter of Lieutenant and Mrs. Price. Fanny Price was at this time just ten years old . . . small of her age . . . exceedingly timid and shy . . . but her air, though awkward, was not vulgar, her voice was sweet, and when she spoke her countenance was pretty. *M.P.*ii.

Price, Frances, *née* Ward, Fanny's mother. Miss Frances married, in the common phrase, to disoblige her family. *M.P.*i.

Price, John and Richard, brothers of Fanny. Two brothers . . . one of whom was a clerk in a public office in London, and the other midshipman on board an Indiaman. *M.P.*xxxviii. (They are named in *M.P.*xxxix.)

Price, Lieutenant, of the Marines, father of Fanny. A Lieutenant of Marines, without education, fortune, or connexions. *M.P.*i. Her father . . . was more negligent of his family, his habits were worse, and his manners coarser, than she had been prepared for. *M.P.*xxxix.

Price, Mary, Fanny's little sister who died. *M.P.*xxxviii.

Price, Sam, brother of Fanny. Sam's voice louder than all the rest ! That boy is fit for a boatswain. *M.P.* xxxviii.

Price, Susan, sister of Fanny. *M.P.*xxxvii. Susan, a well-grown fine girl of fourteen. *M.P.*xxxviii.

Price, Tom and Charles, brothers of Fanny. Two rosy-faced boys, ragged and dirty, about eight and nine years old . . . Tom and Charles. *M.P.*xxxviii.

Price, William, Fanny's eldest and favourite brother. William, the eldest, a year older than herself, her constant companion and friend ; her advocate with her mother (of whom he was the darling) in every distress. *M.P.*ii.

" Pride and Prejudice," was begun in October, 1796, and finished in August, 1797 under the title of *First Impressions.* J.A.'s father wrote on November 1, 1797, to Mr. Cadell, the London publisher, proposing publication, which Cadell declined by return of post, without even seeing the MS. It was published in 1813, as *Pride and Prejudice,* in three volumes, in boards, at 18s., by T. Egerton, Military Library, Whitehall. A second edition appeared the same year, and a third (in two volumes) in 1817.

Prince, Miss, one of Mrs. Goddard's three teachers. *E.*iv.

Prior, M. Some dozen lines of Milton, Pope, and Prior. *N.A.*v. *See* also **Henry and Emma.**

Priory, The, Barton. We will often go to the old ruins of the Priory, and try to trace its foundations. *S.S.* xlvi.

Prospect House, Sanditon. *Sand.* iv.

Pug, Lady Bertram's dog. In vain did Lady Bertram smile and make her sit on the sofa with herself and Pug. *M.P.*ii.

Pulteney Street. *See* **Bath.**

Pump Room. *See* **Bath.**

Pump Yard. *See* **Bath.**

Purvis. I was very much attached to a young man of the name of Purvis. *Watsons*, 299.

Purvis Lodge, near Longbourn. And as for Purvis Lodge, the attics are dreadful. *P.P.*l.

Putney, where the Thorpes lived. *N.A.*xxv.

Pym. The leaders of the Gang, Cromwell, Fairfax, Hampden, and Pym. " H. of E." in *L. & F.* 96.

Pyrenees, The. The Alps and Pyrenees, with their pine forests and their vices. *N.A.*xxv.

Q

" Quarterly Review," The. To lounge away the time as they could, with sofas, and chit-chat, and *Quarterly Reviews. M.P.*x.

Queen, The, in *Henry VIII. M.P.*xxxiv.

Queen Square. *See* **Bath.**

Quick, stage name of Gustavus. *L. & F.* 42.

R

Radcliffe, Mrs. Ann. If I read any it shall be Mrs. Radcliffe's : her novels are amazing enough. *N.A.*vii. *See also* **" Italian, The " " Romance,"** and **" Udolpho."**

Raleigh, Sir Walter. Sir Walter Raleigh . . . is by many people held in great veneration and respect. . . . But as he was an enemy of the noble Essex, I have nothing to say in praise of him. " H. of E." in *L. & F.* 94.

" Rambler, The," quoted. *N.A.*iii. If it be true, as a celebrated writer has maintained, that no young lady can be justified in falling in love before the gentleman's love is declared—*See* a letter from Richardson in .No. 97, Vol. II of *The Rambler*.

Ramsgate. (1) Sir Egerton Brydges said that he had seen J.A. at Ramsgate in 1803. *Life*, 174. (2) Miss Darcy was living at Ramsgate when Wickham planned elopement with her. , *P.P.*xxxv. (3) I went down to Ramsgate for a week with a friend last September. *M.P.*v. *See also* **Albion Place.**

Randalls, the home of the Westons. *E.*i.

Rasselas. *See* **Johnson, Dr.**

Ravenshaw, Lord and Lady. The private theatricals at Ecclesford, the seat of the Right Hon. Lord Ravenshaw, in Cornwall. *M.P.*xiii.

Reading. And wondered whether Mr. Palmer and Colonel Brandon would get farther than Reading that night. *S.S.*xlii. *See* also **Latournelle.**

Rebecca, upper servant in the Prices' house at Portsmouth. *M.P.*xxxviii.

Repton, Mr., an " improver " of grounds and gardens. *M.P.*vi. This was Humphrey Repton, whose *Observations on the Theory and Practice of Landscape Gardening* etc., was published in 1803.

Reynolds, Mrs., housekeeper at Pemberley, Mr. Darcy's seat. The housekeeper came : a respectable-looking elderly woman, much less fine, and more civil, than she [Elizabeth] had any notion of finding her. *P.P.* xliii.

Richard II. " H. of E." in *L. & F.* 85.

Richard III. (1) From Shylock or Richard III down to the singing hero of a farce. *M.P.*xiii. (2) The Character of this Prince has been in general very severely treated by Historians, but as he was a *York,* I am rather inclined to suppose him a very respectable man. " H. of E." in *L. & F.* 87.

Richards, Dr. As the partridges were pretty high, Dr. Richards would have them sent away to the other end of the table. *Watsons,* 338.

Richardson, Miss, one of Mrs. Goddard's three teachers. *E.*iv.

Richardson, Mrs. Mrs. Richardson was come in her coach and would take one of us to Kensington Gardens. *S.S.*xxxviii.

Richardson, Samuel. His fancy had been early caught by all the impassioned and most exceptionable parts of Richardson's [novels]. *Sand.* viii. *See also* **Grandison, Sir Charles, Lovelace,** and **Rambler.**

Richmond, Surrey. (1) They were going to remove immediately to Richmond. *E.*xxxvii. (2) There are some charming little villas about Richmond. *N.A.*xv.

" Rivals, The " [by Sheridan]. *M.P.*xiv.

Rivers Street. *See* **Bath.**

Robert, Dr. Grant's gardener. Here are some of my plants which Robert *will* leave out because the nights are so mild. *M.P.*xxii.

Robertson, Dr., the historian. *N.A.*xiv.

Robertus. " Scraps " in *L. & F.* 139.

Robinson. You like it . . . it is enough. Henry, remember that Robinson is spoken to about it. The cottage remains. *N.A.*xxvi.

Robinson, Mr. You mean what I overheard between him and Mr. Robinson. *P.P.*v.

Robinson, Mr., apothecary at Uppercross. Mr. Robinson felt and felt, and rubbed, and looked grave, and spoke low words both to the father and the aunt. *Pers.* vii.

Roche, Regina Maria. *See* **Children of the Abbey** and **Clermont.**

Roman Emperors. We used to repeat the chronological order . . . of the Roman emperors as low as Severus. *M.P.*ii.

" Romance of the Forest," The. He never read the *Romance of the Forest. E.*iv. This novel, by Ann Radcliffe, was published in 1791.

Rooke, Mrs., nurse and friend of Mrs. Smith, and sister of Mrs. Smith's landlady in Westgate Buildings, Bath. Nurse Rooke thoroughly understands when to speak. She is a shrewd, intelligent, amiable woman. *Pers.* xvii.

Rose, Mr., at Exeter. A prodigious smart young man, quite a beau. *S.S.*xxi.

L

Rosings Park, Lady Catherine de Bourgh's estate. *P.P.*xiv.

Ross, Flora, became Lady Stornoway (*q.v.*).

Ross, Janet. *See* **Fraser.**

Rowling, near Goodnestone, where Edward Austen settled on his first marriage in 1791. "Some of Jane's earliest extant letters were written from Rowling." *Life,* 74.

Roworth, C., Bell yard, Temple-bar, printer of the first edition of *Sense and Sensibility,* three volumes, 1811 ; Vol. I of the first edition of *Pride and Prejudice,* 1813 ; Vol. II of the first edition of *Mansfield Park,* 1814 ; Vols. I and II of the first edition of *Emma,* 1816 ; and Vols. I and II (*Northanger Abbey*) of the first edition of *Northanger Abbey* and *Persuasion,* 1818.

Rushworth, James. A heavy young man, with not more than common sense. *M.P.*iv.

Rushworth, Mrs., his mother. Mrs. Rushworth . . . acknowledged herself very desirous that her son should marry. *M.P.*iv, viii.

Russell, Lady, a widow, friend of Lady Elliot and of Anne Elliot. Lady Russell, of steady age and character, and extremely well provided for. *Pers.* i, v.

Russia. My cousin cannot tell the principal rivers in Russia. *M.P.*ii.

S

Sackville Street. *See* **London.**

St. Clair, Lord. His wife was Laurina and their four daughters, Claudia, Matilda, Bertha and Agatha were the respective mothers of Laura, Sophia, Philander, and Gustavus. *L. & F.* 22.

St. Clement's. *See* **London.**

St. Domingo. Captain Frederick Wentworth . . . being made commander in consequence of the action off St. Domingo. [1806.] *Pers.* iv.

St. George's, Fields. *See* **London.**

St. George's, Hanover Square. *See* **London.**

St. Ives, Lord. Lord St. Ives, whose father we all know to have been a country curate, without bread to eat. *Pers.* iii.

St. James's Street. *See* **London.**

St. John's College, Oxford, at which George Austen (J.A.'s father) held a scholarship and later a Fellowship.

St. Paul's. *See* **London.**

Salisbury. We have very good shops in Salisbury. *N.A.* iii.

Sally, under-servant in the Prices' house. She had been into the kitchen . . . to hurry Sally and help make the toast. *M.P.* xxxviii.

Sallyport, The, Portsmouth. The three boys . . . determined to see their brother and Mr. Campbell to the Sallyport. *M.P.* xxxviii.

Sam, Old—at the Hotel, Sanditon. She was directing the Disposal of the Luggage, and helping old Sam uncover the Trunks. *Sand*. ix.

Sandcroft Hill. When we got to the bottom of Sandcroft Hill . . . I got out and walked up. *M.P.*xx.

Sandersons, The. The Parrys and Sandersons luckily are coming to-night, you know, and that will amuse her. *S.S.*xxx.

" Sanditon "—the fragment of a novel, written in January to March, 1817, shortly before the death of the author. It seems pretty certainly to be only a first draft. It was first printed from the MS. in 1925, and was published by the Clarendon Press, Oxford. The MS. had no title, but the fragment had long been known to members of the family as *Sanditon*.

Sanditon. A young and rising Bathing-place, certainly the favourite spot of all that are to be found along the Coast of Sussex. *Sand*. i.

Sanditon Church. The Church and neat village of Sanditon. *Sand*. iv.

Sanditon House, the residence of Lady Denham. *Sand*. iv.

Sarah, one of Mrs. Bennet's two housemaids. Here, Sarah, come to Miss Bennet this moment, and help her on with her gown. *P.P.*lv.

Sarah, the old nursery-maid of the Musgrove family. *Pers.* xiii.

Saunders, John. I meant to take them over to John Saunders the first thing I did. *E.*xxvii.

Scarlets, in Wargrave parish, Berkshire, the estate of James Leigh Perrot (*q.v.*).

Scheherazade, The Sultaness. Mr. Elliot's character, like the Sultaness Scheherazade's head, must live another day. *Pers.* xxiii.

Scholey, Old. Old Scholey ran in at breakfast time, to say she had slipped her moorings and was coming out. *M.P.*xxxviii.

" School for Scandal, The " [by Sheridan]. *M.P.*xiv.

Scotland. (1) We were within a few hours of eloping together for Scotland. *S.S.*xxxi. (2) Julia's elopement ; she is gone to Scotland with Yates. *M.P.*xlvi. (3) Your friend Mr. Graham's intending to have a bailiff from Scotland, to look after his new estate. *E.*xii. (4) *L. & F.* 21. (5) My Brother will leave Scotland in a few days. "Les. C." in *L. & F.* 49.

Scotland, The King of. "H. of E." in *L. & F.* 88.

Scotland. The Queen of [Mary]. That noble Duke of Norfolk who was so warm in the Queen of Scotland's cause. *Ibid.* 89.

Scott [Sir Walter]. (1) You know what he thinks of Cowper and Scott. *S.S.*x. (2) Talking as before of Mr. Scott and Lord Byron. *Pers.* xii. (3) Do you remember, said he, Scott's beautiful Lines on the Sea ? *Sand.* vii.

See also **" Lady of Branxholm Hall "** ; **" Lady of the Lake "** ; **" Lay of the Last Minstrel "** ; and **" Marmion."**

" Scraps " printed for the first time, with other Juvenilia, in *Love and Freindship*, 1922 (pp. 127–140.)

Scroggs, Miss, a visitor at Sanditon. *Sand.* iv.

Scudamore, Lady. Happy Lady Scudamore to live within a mile of the divine Henrietta ! " C. of L." in *L. & F.* 117.

Seaton, Colonel, *Ibid.* 106.

" Sense and Sensibility " was first written in letters, in the Richardson manner, under the title of *Elinor and Marianne*—at what date is unknown. (*Life,* 80.) In its present form *Sense and Sensibility* was written after *First Impressions*, the first form of *Pride and Prejudice*, but was Jane Austen's first published novel. It was begun in November, 1797 (*Mem.* iii) but nothing more is known of it till 1811, when J. was in London, correcting the proofs. It was published in that year in three volumes—" By a Lady," said the title-page—by T. Egerton, Whitehall. The book was priced 15s. in boards. " Every copy . . . is sold," wrote the author on July 3, 1813 . . . " it has brought me £140, besides the copyright, if that should ever be of any value." The second edition appeared in 1813.

Serle, the Woodhouses' cook. Serle understands boiling an egg better than anybody. *E.*iii.

Sevenoaks, Kent. (1) George Austen (1) (*q.v.*) " was of a family long established in the neighbourhood of Tenterden and Sevenoaks in Kent." (*Mem.* i.) (2) J.A. and C. with their parents, visited their great uncle Francis Austen at Sevenoaks, in 1788. (*Life,* 58.)

Severus, Roman emperor. We used to repeat the

chronological order . . . of the Roman emperors as low as Severus. *M.P.*ii.

Sewell's Farm, near Thornton Lacey. *M.P.*xxv.

Shakespeare. (1) A book on the table which had the air of being very recently closed, a volume of Shakespeare. *M.P.*xxxiv. (2)—a quotation. *N.A.*i. (3) A very agreeable woman by Shakespeare's account. "H. of E." in *L. & F.* 85.
See also " **Hamlet,**" " **Macbeth,**" and " **Othello.**"

Sharpe, Martha. A year or two back, when Martha Sharpe and I had so many secrets together. *S.S.* xxxviii.

Shaw, Mrs. I considered her engagement to Mrs. Shaw just at that time as very unfortunate for me. *Watsons,* 301.

Sheldon, Mrs. I happened to be calling on Mrs. Sheldon when her coachman sprained his foot. *Sand.* v.

Shepherd, John, lawyer and agent to Sir Walter Elliot. *Pers.* i. Mr. Shepherd laughed, as he knew he must, at this wit. *Pers.* iii.

Sheridan [Richard Brinsley]. " Mr. Sheridan's play of the *Critic,* where they will find many interesting ancedotes " of Sir Walter Raleigh. " H. of E." in *L. & F.* 95.
See also " **Critic,**" " **Rivals,**" and " **School for Scandal.**"

Shirley, Rev. Dr., rector of Uppercross. Dr. Shirley, the rector, who for more than forty years had been zealously discharging all the duties of his office. *Pers.* ix.

Shirley, Mrs., his wife. It is the best thing he could do, both for himself and Mrs. Shirley. *Pers.* xii.

Shore, Jane. " H. of E." in *L. & F.* 86.

Shropshire, (1) the county in which Captain Wentworth's brother had settled. *Pers.* ix. (2) How should I know in Shropshire what is passing of that nature in Surrey ? *Watsons,* 306.

Shylock. (1) J.A. saw Kean in Shylock at Drury Lane Theatre in March, 1814. (*Life,* 294.) (2) I could be fool enough at this moment to undertake any character . . . from Shylock or Richard III down to the singing hero of a farce. *M.P.*xiii.

Sicily. A very pretty amber cross which William had brought her from Sicily. *M.P.*xxvi.

Sidmouth, Devon, (1) visited by the Austens in the summer of 1801. (*Life,* 172.) (2) Yes, sir, a Mr. Elliot . . . came in last night from Sidmouth. *Pers.* xii.

Sidney, G., Northumberland Street, Strand, printer of Vols. II and III of the first edition of *Pride and Prejudice,* 1813 ; and Vols. I and III of the first edition of *Mansfield Park,* 1814.

Simnel, Lambert. If Perkin Warbeck was really the Duke of York, why might not Lambert Simnel be the Widow of Richard ? " H. of E." in *L. & F.* 87.

Simpson, Mr., of Exeter. A prodigious smart young man, quite a beau, clerk to Mr. Simpson, you know. *S.S.*xxi.

Sion Hill. *See* **Bath.**

Skinner, Dr. A neighbour of ours, Dr. Skinner, was

here for his health last winter, and came away quite stout. *N.A*.viii.

Skinners, The. The Skinners were here [Bath] last year —I wish they were here now. *N.A*.ii.

Sleath, Eleanor. *See* **Orphan of the Rhine.**

Sloane Street. *See* **London.**

Smallridge, Mrs.—Charming woman—most superior. *E*.xliv.

Smith, Charles, the deceased husband of Mrs. Smith, *née* Hamilton (*q.v.*) My poor Charles, who had the finest, most generous spirit in the world. *Pers*. xxi.

Smith, Charles. *Lady S.* Lett. 4.

Smith, Harriet. The natural daughter of somebody. . . . She was short, plump, and fair, with a fine bloom, blue eyes, light hair, regular features, and a look of great sweetness. *E*.iii.

Smith, John. Publishing the banns of marriage between John Smith and Mary Brown. *S.S*.xli.

Smith, Lieutenant, R.N., a visitor at Sanditon. *Sand.* vi.

Smith, Miss, an acquaintance of Mrs. Hughes. *N.A*.x.

Smith, Mr., of Compton, a friend of James Rushworth. Smith has not much above a hundred acres altogether in his grounds, which is little enough. *M.P*.vi.

Smith, Mrs., *née* Hamilton, an old schoolfellow of Anne Elliot. She was a widow and poor. . . . She had had difficulties of every sort to contend with, and in addition . . . had been afflicted with a severe rheumatic fever. *Pers*. xvii.

Smith, Mrs., of Allenham Court, a cousin of Willoughby. *S.S.*xiii.

Smythe, Arabella. "Scraps" in *L. & F.* 132.

Sneyd, Mr ; Mr. Sneyd, Junior ; Mrs. Sneyd ; Miss Sneyd ; Miss Augusta Sneyd. My friend Sneyd . . . his father and mother and sisters were there, all near to me. *M.P.*v.

Somerset, The Duke of, Protector of the Realm. This Man was on the whole of a very amiable Character. "H. of E." in *L. & F.* 90.

Somerset, The Earl of [Robert Carr]. The principal favourites of his Majesty were Car [*sic*], who was afterwards created Earl of Somerset. . . . "H. of E." in *L. & F.* 95.

Somersetshire. (1) He has a pretty little estate of his own in Somersetshire. *S.S.*ix. (2) The county of Kellynch and Uppercross. *Pers.* i.

Sonning, Berkshire. *See* **Cooper.**

Sophia, a "young lady crossed in love." "C. of L." in *L. & F.* 107.

Sophia, the wife of "Edward's most particular freind," and granddaughter of Lord St. Clair (*q.v.*). *L. & F.* 15.

Sotherton Court, the home of the Rushworths. Sotherton Court is the noblest old place in the world. *M.P.*vi.

Southampton. (1) Jane Austen, in very early life, spent a short time at Southampton, with her sister, under the care of Mrs. Cawley (*q.v*). In the autumn of 1806 Mrs. Austen and her daughters moved from Bath to Southampton, the Rev. George Austen having died in 1805. After a few months spent in lodgings, "they resided in a commodious old-fashioned house in a corner of Castle Square." (*Mem.* iv.) They lived there till April, 1809, when they went by way of Alton to Bookham, and thence to Godmersham, on visits, settling at Chawton in September of that year. (2) Beware of the . . . stinking fish of Southampton. *L. & F. 7.*

South End, Essex. It was an awkward business, my dear, your spending the autumn at South End instead of coming here. I never had much opinion of the sea air. *E.*xii.

South Foreland. The noblest expanse of Ocean between the South foreland and the Land's end. *Sand.* iv.

Spain. I was born in Spain and received my Education at a Convent in France. *L. & F.* 6.

Spain, Philip, King of. " H. of E." in *L. & F.* 91.

Spangle, Sir Edward. *The Mystery* in *Mem.* iii.

Sparks, Miss. I had it from Miss Sparks myself. *S.S.*xxxviii.

" Spectator, The." *N.A.*v.

Speed, Mrs., Mrs. Smith's landlady at Bath. *Pers.* xxi.

Spicers, The. Charles has a very fair chance, through the Spicers, of getting something from the Bishop in the course of a year or two. *Pers.* ix.

Spithead. She had a letter from him herself . . . sent into Portsmouth, with the first boat that left the *Antwerp*, at anchor, in Spithead. *M.P.*xxiv.

Staffordshire. Mr. Vernon I think was a great deal too kind to her, when he was in Staffordshire. *Lady S.,* Lett. 3.

Staines. " Scraps " in *L. & F.* 135.

Stanhill, the house from which the Dashwoods moved to Norland Park. *S.S.*ii.

Stanhope, Admiral, a Bath acquaintance of J.A.—" a gentlemanlike man, but then his legs are too short, and his tail too long." *(Life,* 168.)

Stanley, Sir Thomas. " C. of L." in *L. & F.* 113.

Stanly, Mr. To-morrow Mr. Stanly's family will drink tea with us. *Ibid.* 103.

Stanton, Surrey. Nor guess at the object which could take her away from Stanton just as you were coming home. *Watsons,* 301.

Stanton Wood. They will throw off at Stanton Wood on Wednesday at nine o'clock. *Ibid.* 342.

Stanwix Lodge, near Mansfield. I shall let Everingham, and rent a place in this neighbourhood ; perhaps Stanwix Lodge. *M.P.*xxx.

Staves, Gregory, a staymaker, reputed father of Gustavus. *L. & F.* 39.

Steele, Anne. The eldest, who was nearly thirty, with a very plain and not a sensible face. *S.S.*xxi.

Steele, Lucy, her younger sister, who married Robert Ferrars. Lucy is monstrous pretty, and so good-humoured and agreeable. *S.S.*xxi.

Steele, Mr., their father. *S.S.*xxxviii.

Stent, Mrs., an early acquaintance of J.A. Poor Mrs. Stent ! it has been her lot to be always in the way ; but we must be merciful, for perhaps in time we may come to be Mrs. Stents ourselves, unequal to anything, and unwelcome to everybody. Letter of J. to C. in *Mem.* iv ; *Life*, 186.

Stephen, a groom at Mansfield Park. You know how steady Stephen is. *M.P.*xx.

Sterne.   A paper from the *Spectator*, and a chapter from Sterne. *N.A.*v.

Stevenson, Elizabeth, maiden name of Lady Elliot (*q.v.*)

Stevenson, James, of South Park, Gloucestershire, father-in-law of Sir Walter Elliot. *Pers.* i.

Steventon, Hants., of which parish, with Deane, little more than a mile away, George Austen, Jane's father, was rector.   Jane was born at the Parsonage, December 16, 1775, and spent the first twenty-five years of her life there.   Steventon is a small village in a valley about seven miles south of Basingstoke. " It is difficult to find Steventon, so little is there of it, and that so much scattered ; a few cottages, a farm, and beyond, half a mile away, the church, with a pump in a field near to mark the site of the old rectory house where Jane Austen was born.   This is all that remains of her time." (G. E. Mitton, *Jane Austen and Her Times*, Ch. i.)

Stirling.   Philippa . . . generally accompanied him in his little Excursions to Sterling [*sic*]. *L. & F.* 38.

Stoke.   I will take my horse early to-morrow morning, and ride over to Stoke. *M.P.*xv.

Stoke, The Great House at, near Longbourn. Haye Park might do . . . or the great house at Stoke, if the drawing-room were larger. *P.P.*l.

Stokes, Jack. I have begun my letter ; Jack Stokes is to call for it to-morrow. *Watsons,* 334.

Stokes, Mrs., landlady of the Crown Inn, Highbury. If I could be sure of the rooms being thoroughly aired— but is Mrs. Stokes to be trusted ? *E.*xxix.

Stone, Mr. My uncle was called away upon business to that horrid man Mr. Stone. *P.P.*li.

Stoneleigh Abbey was visited by J., with her sister and mother, after their Bath home was broken up in 1805.

Stornoway, Flora, Lady, *née* Ross. Who jilted a very nice young man in the Blues, for the sake of that horrid Lord Stornoway. *M.P.*xxxvi.

Stornoway, Lord. That horrid Lord Stornoway who has about as much sense, Fanny, as Mr. Rushworth, but much worse-looking, and with a blackguard character. *M.P.*xxxvi.

Strafford, Earl of. " H. of E." in *L. & F.* 96.

Strafford family, The. Mr. Wentworth was nobody, I remember . . . nothing to do with the Strafford family. *Pers.* iii.

Streatham, where J.A. visited Mrs. Hill (Catharine Bigg) in 1811. *Life,* 251.

Strephon, a character in " The First Act of a Comedy." " Scraps " in *L. & F.* 133.

Stringer. " Old Stringer and his son," gardeners. *Sand.* iv.

Stuarts, The. To forget the Adoration which as *Stuarts* it was their Duty to pay them. " H. of E." in *L. & F.* 96.

Styles, Mr. *Watsons,* 328.

Suckling, Mr., the rich brother-in-law of Mrs. Elton. Maple Grove, My brother Mr. Suckling's seat . . . Mr. Suckling is extremely fond of exploring. *E.*xxxii.

Suckling, Old Mr., his father. I am almost sure that old Mr. Suckling had completed the purchase before his death. *E.*xxxvi.

Suckling, Selina, *née* Hawkins, wife of Mr. Suckling and sister of Mrs. Elton. *E.*xxxii.

Suffolk. " C. of L." in *L. & F.* 115.

Suffolk, The Duke of. " H. of E." in *L. & F.* 88.

Summers, Miss. Head of a school in Wigmore Street. *Lady S.,* Lett. 2.

Sun, The, an inn room. " Scraps " in *L. & F.* 133.

Surrey, (1) the county of Highbury. *E.*xi. (2) A rich West Indian from Surrey. *Sand.* v. (3) The first winter assembly in the town of D. in Surrey. *Watsons,* 297.

Susan, supposed to be the original title of *Northanger Abbey.* *Life,* 174.

Sussex. (1) The family of Dashwood had been long settled in Sussex. *S.S.*i. (2) Mr. Vernon's invitation to prolong his stay in Sussex that they may have some hunting together. *Lady S.,* Lett. 8. (3) I live in Perthshire, you in Susex. " Les. C." in *L. & F.* 49.

Sussex Coast, The. *Sand.* i.

Swisserland. They were looking over views in Swisserland. *E*.xlii.

Switzerland. Italy, Switzerland and the South of France might be as fruitful in horrors as they were there represented. *N.A.*xxv.

Sydney Gardens. *See* **Bath.**

Sydney Place. *See* **Bath.**

T

Talbot. *See* **Lindsay.**

" Task, The," by Cowper. Allusions (1) Bk iv. l. 290. *E*.xli. (2) Bk. i. l. 318. *M.P.*vi.

Tattersal's. *See* **London.**

Taunton. With whom he shortly afterwards fell into company in attending the quarter sessions at Taunton. *Pers.* iii.

Taylor, Miss Anne, Emma's governess, companion and friend, who became Mr. Weston's second wife. *See* **Weston, Mrs.**

Taylor, Mrs. Mrs. Taylor told me of it half an hour ago. *S.S.*xxx.

Teignmouth, Devon. The Austens were probably there in 1802. *Life,* 173.

Temple, The. *See* **London.**

Tenterden. George Austen (*q.v.*), J.A.'s father, " was of a family long established in the neighbourhood of Tenterden and Sevenoaks in Kent." *Mem.* i.

Terrace, The, Sanditon. One short row of smart-looking Houses, called the Terrace, with a broad walk in front, aspiring to be the Mall of the Place. *Sand.* iv.

Tetbury. It was only ten o'clock when we came from Tetbury. *N.A.*vii.

Teuthold, P. *See* **Necromancer.**

" Texel," The, a ship. Old Scholey . . . thought you would be sent first to the *Texel*. *M.P.*xxxviii.

Thomas, man-servant at Barton Cottage. Who . . . [was] just beginning an inquiry of Thomas as to the source of his intelligence. *S.S.*xlvii.

Thomson, James, the poet of " The Seasons." (1) Thomson, Cowper, Scott . . . she would buy them all over and over again. *S.S.*xvii. (2) quoted, *N.A.*i.

Thornberry Park. He was really going to his friends at Thornberry Park for the whole day to-morrow. *Pers.* xxii.

Thornton Lacey, Edmund Bertram's first cure. Thornton Lacey was the name of his impending living, as Miss Crawford well knew. *M.P.*xxv.

Thorpe, Anne, Isabella and Maria, middle, eldest and youngest daughters of Mrs. Thorpe. [Mrs. Thorpe's] eldest daughter had great personal beauty ; and the

K

younger ones, by pretending to be as handsome as their sister, imitating her air, and dressing in the same style, did very well. *N.A.*iv.

Thorpe, Edward and William, second and third sons of Mrs. Thorpe. Edward [was] at Merchant Taylors', and William at sea. *N.A.*iv.

Thorpe, John, eldest son. *N.A.*iv. He was a stout young man, of middling height, who, with a plain face and ungraceful form, seemed fearful of being too handsome unless he wore the dress of a groom. *N.A*.vii.

Thorpe, Mrs., a former schoolfellow and intimate of Mrs. Allen. A good-humoured, well-meaning woman, and a very indulgent mother. *N.A.*iv.

"Thrush," The, H.M. Sloop, of which William Price was made Second-Lieutenant. *M.P.*xxxi.

Tilney, Eleanor, sister of Henry. Miss Tilney had a good figure, a pretty face, and a very agreeable countenance. . . . Her manners showed good sense and good breeding. *N.A.*viii.

Tilney, Frederick, Captain in the 12th Light Dragoons, elder son of General Tilney. *N.A.*xiv. A very fashionable-looking, handsome young man. *N.A*.xvi.

Tilney, General, father of Eleanor, Frederick and Henry. A very handsome man, of a commanding aspect, past the bloom, but not past the vigour of life. *N.A.*x.

Tilney, Henry. He seemed to be about four or five and twenty, was rather tall, had a pleasing countenance, a very intelligent and lively eye, and, if not quite handsome, was very near it. *N.A.*iii.

Tilney, Mrs., *née* Drummond, the deceased wife of General Tilney. Mrs. Tilney was a Miss Drummond . . . a very large fortune. *N.A.*ix.

Tintern Abbey, in a window transparency. *M.P.*xvi.

"Tirocinium," Cowper's, alluded to—With what intense desire she wants her home—see line 562. *M.P.*xlv.

Tom, had been sent off immediately for the Crown chaise. *E.*xliv.

Tombuctoo [*sic*].   He felt a strong curiosity to ascertain whether the Neighbourhood of Tombuctoo might not afford some solitary House adapted for Clara's reception. *Sand.* viii.

" Tom Jones " [by Fielding, 1749]. [John Thorpe *loq.*]. There has not been a tolerably decent one [novel] come out since *Tom Jones,* except the *Monk. N.A.*vii.

Tomlinson, James, query, the son of Mr. Tomlinson. *Watsons,* 328.

Tomlinson, Mr.   If Mr. Tomlinson, the banker, might be indulged in calling his newly-erected house at the end of the town, with a shrubbery and sweep, in the country. *Watsons,* 307.

Tomlinson, Mrs., his wife. *Watsons,* 328.

"Tour to the Highlands," Gilpin's. Her curiosity to behold the delightful scenes . . . had been so much raised by Gilpin's *Tour to the Highlands. L. & F.* 37.   *See* **Gilpin.**

κ*

Tower, The. *See* **London.**

Trafalgar, Battle of. Admiral Croft . . . was in the Trafalgar action. *Pers.* iii.

Trafalgar House, Mr. Parker's abode. I almost wish I had not named Trafalgar for Waterloo is more the thing now. *Sand.* iv.

Trent. I remember no gentleman resident at Monkford since the time of old Governor Trent. *Pers.* iii.

Tunbridge, (1) where Francis Austen, uncle of George Austen (1) (*q.v.*) lived. (2) I do not call Tunbridge or Cheltenham the country. *M.P.*xxi. (3) She could compare the balls of Bath with those of Tunbridge. *N.A.*iv. (4) *Sand.* i. (5) We might meet at Bath, at Tunbridge, or anywhere else indeed, could we but be at the same place together. " Les. C." in *L. & F.* 49.

Tunbridge School, where George Austen (1) was educated.

Tunbridge Wells (1) This was the letter, directed to " Charles Smith, Esq., Tunbridge Wells." *Pers.* xxi. (2) An occasional month at Tunbridge Wells. *Sand.* ii.

Tupman. People of the name of Tupman, very lately· settled there, and encumbered with many low connexions, but giving themselves immense airs, and expecting to be on a footing with the old-established families. *E.*xxxvi.

Turner, Mr., the first husband of Emma Watson's aunt, Mrs. O'Brien. *Watsons,* 312.

Turner's, at Portsmouth. I have been to Turner's

about your mess ; it is all in a way to be done.   *M.P.* xxxviii.

Tuscany. Oh, that we had such weather here as they had at Udolpho, or at least in Tuscany.   *N.A.*xi.

Twickenham. The Admiral . . . bought a cottage at Twickenham for us all to spend our summers in. *M.P.*vi.

U

" **Udolpho, The Mysteries of** " [by Ann Radcliffe, 1794]. While I have *Udolpho* to read, I feel as if nobody could make me miserable.   *N.A.*vi.

Union Passage and **Union Street.**   *See* **Bath.**

Up Lyme, near Lyme Regis.   The woody varieties of the cheerful village of Up Lyme.   *Pers.* xi.

Uppercross, a village in Somerset.   *Pers.* i.   A moderate-sized village which a few years back had been completely in the old English style. *Pers.* v.

Uppercross Cottage, the residence of the Charles Musgroves. A farmhouse elevated into a cottage . . . with its veranda. French windows, and other prettinesses. *Pers.* v.

Uppercross Great House, or **Mansion House** (ch. ix.) the residence of the senior Musgroves.   The mansion of the squire, with its high walls, great gates, and old trees, substantial and unmodernised. *Pers.* v.

Upper Rooms. *See* **Bath.**

Upper Seymour Street. *See* **London.**

Usk, The Vale of, Wales. Our mansion was situated in one of the most romantic parts of the Vale of Usk. *L. & F.* 6.

V

Vauxhall. *See* **London.**

Venice. They had only accomplished some views of St. Mark's Place, Venice, when Frank Churchill entered the room. *E.*xlii.

Vernon, Catherine (1) daughter of Lady De Courcy and wife of Charles Vernon. *Lady S.*, Lett. 1. She is perfectly well bred indeed, and has the air of a woman of fashion. Lett. 5.

Vernon Catherine (2), her daughter. Sweet little Catherine. *Lady S.*, Lett. 20.

Vernon, Charles, husband of Catherine (1) and brother of Lady Susan. *Lady S.*, Lett. i.

Vernon, Frederic, his son. A young Frederic, whom I take on my lap, and sigh over for his dear Uncle's sake. *Lady S.*, Lett. 5.

Vernon, Frederica Susanna, daughter of Lady Susan. I shall deposit her [F.S.V.] under the care of Miss Summers in Wigmore Street, till she becomes a little more reasonable. *Lady S.,* Lett. 2.

Vernon, Lady Susan. *Lady S.,* Lett. 1. The most accomplished Coquette in England. Lett. 4. Delicately fair, with fine grey eyes and dark eyelashes. Lett. 6.

Vernon, Mr., Lady Susan's deceased husband. *Lady S.,* Lett. 6.

Vernon Castle. *Lady S.,* Lett. 5.

Vicarage Lane, Highbury. Vicarage Lane, a lane leading at right-angles from the broad, though irregular, main street of the place. *E.*x.

Vicarage, The, Highbury. An old and not very good house. *E.* x.

"Vicar of Wakefield, The," Goldsmith's. I know he has read the *Vicar of Wakefield*. *E.*iv.

Villiers, George, Duke of Buckingham. " H. of E." in *L. & F.* 95.

" Visit, The," an early sketch. *Life,* 57.

Voltaire. That line of the Poet Cowper in his description of the religious Cottager, as opposed to Voltaire— " *She,* never heard of half a mile from home." *Sand.* i.

W

Walcot, near Bath. He had not turned a hair till we came to Walcot church. *N.A.*vii.

Wales. (1) My Father was a native of Ireland, and an inhabitant of Wales. *L. & F.* 6. (2) [Wales] which is a principality contiguous to England. " Scraps " in *L. & F.* 138.

Wales, The Prince of. *Ibid.* 138.

Walker, Miss. *S.S.*xxx.

Wallis, Colonel, friend of Mr. W. W. Elliot. Colonel Wallis, a highly respectable man, perfectly the gentleman (and not an ill-looking man, Sir Walter added). *Pers.* xv, xx.

Wallis, Mrs., his wife. Mr. Elliot spoke of her as " a most charming woman, quite worthy of being known in Camden Place." *Pers.* xv. The beautiful Mrs Wallis. *Pers.* xvi.

Wallis, Mrs., baker at Highbury. Then the baked apples came home ; Mrs. Wallis sent them by her boy. *E.*xxvii.

Walsh, Captain. Captain Walsh thinks you will certainly have a cruise to the westward. *M.P.*xxxviii.

Walsingham, Sir Francis. " H. of E." in *L. & F.* 91.

Warbeck, Perkin. *Ibid.* 87.

Ward, Frances, younger sister of Maria, married— Price, " a Lieutenant of Marines, without education, fortune, or connexions." *See* **Price, Mrs.**

Ward, Maria, of Huntingdon, niece of a lawyer, became Lady Bertram (*q.v.*)

Ward, Miss, elder sister of Maria, *m.* the Rev. Mr. Norris. *See* **Norris, Mrs.**

Wargrave. *See* **Scarlets.**

Warleigh, Mrs. Cope's house. " C. of L." in *L. & F.* 104.

Warwick. *P.P.*xlii .

Warwick, The Earl of. Perkin Warbeck . . . was beheaded with the Earl of Warwick. " H. of E." in *L. & F.* 88.

Waterloo. Mr. Parker wished he had not named his house Trafalgar—" for Waterloo is more the thing now." *Sand.* iv.

Waterloo Crescent, Sanditon. *Sand.* iv.

Watson, Augusta, the little daughter of Robert and Jane Watson. It went very hard with Augusta to have us come away without her. *Watsons,* 346.

Watson, Elizabeth, daughter of Mr. Watson. Whose delight in a ball was not lessened by a ten years' enjoyment. *Ibid.* 298.

Watson, Emma, daughter of Mr. Watson. Who was very recently returned to her family from the care of an aunt who had brought her up. *Ibid.* 297, 298.

Watson, Jane, wife of Robert. *Ibid.* 344. Mrs. Robert . . . gave genteel parties and wore fine clothes . . . her manners were pert and conceited. *Ibid.* 345.

Watson, Margaret, daughter of Mr. Watson. *Ibid.* 301.

Margaret was not without beauty ; she had a slight pretty figure, and rather wanted countenance than good features. *Watsons*, 345.

Watson, Mr. Was sickly and had lost his wife. *Ibid.* 297, 337.

Watson, Penelope, daughter of Mr. Watson. Penelope . . . thinks everything fair for a husband. *Ibid.* 299.

Watson, Robert, son of Mr. Watson. *Ibid.* 299. Robert Watson was an attorney at Croydon in a good way of business. *Ibid.* 345.

Watson, Sam, son of Mr. Watson, a surgeon. *Ibid.* 305.

Watson, Miss. Colonel Forster and Captain Carter do not go so often to Miss Watson's as they did when they first came. *P.P.*vii.

"Watsons, The," " must have been written during the author's residence in Bath." [1801–1805.] (*Mem.* iv.) It was first printed as an appendix to the second edition, 1871, of J. E. Austen-Leigh's *Memoir*.

Weald, The, Sussex. On the other side of Battel— quite down in the Weald. *Sand.* i.

Webbs, The Miss. The Miss Webbs all play, and their father has not so good an income as yours. *P.P.*xxix.

Wentworth, Edward, curate of Monkford. Mr. Wentworth . . . had the curacy of Monkford, you know, Sir Walter, some time back, for two or three years. *Pers.* iii.

Wentworth, Frederick, Captain in the Navy, brother to

Edward.   A remarkably fine young man, with a great deal of intelligence, spirit, and brilliancy. *Pers.* iv, vii.

Wentworth, Sophia, his sister, *m.* Admiral Croft. *See* **Croft, Mrs.**

Werter, The sorrows of.   We were convinced he had no soul, that he had never read the sorrows of Werter. *L. & F.* 24.

Westbrook.   " C. of L." in *L. & F.* 103.

Westerham, Kent, near which were Hunsford Parsonage and Rosings Park. *P.P.*xiii.

Western Islands, The.   A friend of mine and I had such a lovely cruise together off the Western Islands. *Pers.* viii.

Westgate Buildings. *See* **Bath.**

West Hall.   A year and a half is the very utmost that they can have lived at West Hall. *E.*xxxvi.

West Indian, A rich, from " Surry." *Sand.* v.

West Indies.   (1) Was there any chance of his being hereafter useful to Sir Thomas in the concerns of his West Indian property ? *M.P.*i. (2) We do not call Bermuda or Bahama, you know, the West Indies. *Pers.* viii.

Westminster and **Westminster School.** *See* **London.**

Weston, near Bath, to which J.A. walked. *Life,* 168.

Weston, Anne, *née* Taylor.   She had been a friend and companion such as few possessed : intelligent, well-informed, useful, gentle. . . .   *E.*i, v.

Weston, Anna, her baby daughter. *E*.liii.

Weston, Frank. *See* **Churchill, Frank.**

Weston, Mr., ex-captain, who married Miss Taylor as his second wife. A man of unexceptionable character, easy fortune, suitable age, and pleasant manners. *E*.i, xiv.

Westons, The. The Westons will be with us, and it will be quite delightful. *S.S.*xx.

Weymouth. (1) I was with my uncle at Weymouth. *S.S.*xx.   (2) To tell of races at Weymouth, and parties and friends. *M.P.*xii.   (3) *E*. xi.

Whaddon, near Bath. *See* **Cooper.**

" Wheel of Fortune, The." *M.P.*xiv. A comedy by Richard Cumberland, produced at Covent Garden in 1795.

Whitaker, Mr., apparently a friend or acquaintance of J.A. " H. of E." in *L. & F.* 92.

Whitaker, Mrs., Mrs. Rushworth's housekeeper. Nothing would satisfy that good old Mrs. Whitaker but my taking one of the cheeses. *M.P.*x.

Whitakers, The. Who is to dance ? Who ? why yourselves and the Careys and Whitakers, to be sure. *S.S.*xviii.

Whitby, Miss, daughter of Mrs. Whitby. Miss Whitby . . . with all her glossy curls and smart Trinkets. *Sand.* vi.

Whitby, Mrs. Mrs. Whitby at the Library was sitting

in her inner room, reading one of her own Novels, for want of employment. *Sand.* vi.

Whitby.   A young Whitby running off with 5 vols. under his arm to Sir Edward's Gig. *Sand.* viii.

Whitby's—a shop at Sanditon. You can get a Parasol at Whitby's for little Mary at any time. *Sand.* iv.

White Hart Inn, The.   *See* **Bath.**

White Hart Inn, The, at D. where balls were held. *Watsons,* 307.

White House, The, Mansfield, where Mrs. Norris lived. I am to leave Mansfield Park, and go to the White House, I suppose, as soon as she is removed there. *M.P.*iii.

Whitwell.   A very fine place about twelve miles from Barton, belonging to a brother-in-law of Colonel Brandon. *S.S.*xii.

Wickham, George, an officer. His appearance was greatly in his favour ; he had all the best parts of beauty, a fine countenance, a good figure, and very pleasing address. *P.P.*xv.

Wickham, Mr., his father, deceased, who had been steward to Mr. Darcy's father. *P.P.*xviii.

Wick Rocks.   *See* **Bath.**

Wickstead, Mr. Howard's parish. *Watsons,* 321.

Widcombe, to which J.A. walked. *Life,* 169.

Wigmore Street.   *See* **London.**

Wilcox, the Bertrams' coachman, who admired Miss Crawford's horsemanship. *M.P.*vii. The name appears in ch. viii.

Wildenheim, Baron, a character in *Lovers' Vows* (*q.v.*). *M.P.*xiv.

Wilhelminus. " Scraps " in *L. & F.* 139.

Will, Peter. *See* **Horrid Mysteries.**

William, servant to General Tilney. *N.A.*xiii.

William, servant to Edward Lindsay. I mounted my Horse and followed by my faithful William set forwards for my Aunts. *L. & F.* 9, 10.

William, the Lutterells' servant. "Les. C." in *L. & F.* 52.

Williams, Eliza, natural daughter of Mrs. Eliza Brandon (*q.v.*). *S.S.*xiii (also xxxi and xxxii.)

Williams, Maria. A young lady in distressed circumstances. " C. of L." in *L. & F.* 114.

Williams, Mrs., her mother. Mrs. Williams is too wise to be extravagant. *Ibid.* 111.

Williams, Sir Thomas. *See* **Cooper, Edward and Jane.**

Willingden and **Willingden Abbots,** Sussex. *Sand.* i.

Willoughby, Edward. Can it be that I have a greater affection for Willoughby than I had for his amiable predecessors ? " C. of L." in *L. & F.* 105.

Willoughby, John, of Combe Magna. His manly beauty and more than common gracefulness were instantly the theme of general admiration. *S.S.*ix.

Wilson, Lady Susan Vernon's maid. *Lady S.*, Lett. 23.

Wiltshire, the county of Fullerton, the Morlands' village.
*N.A.*i.

Wimpole Street. *See* **London.**

Winchester. J.A. visited Mrs. Heathcote and Miss
Bigg at Winchester in 1814. She was conveyed to
Winchester, when very ill, on May 24, 1817, and died
there July 18, 1817. She and her sister lodged in
College Street. (*Life*, 388, 389, and 394.) She was
buried in Winchester Cathedral.

Windsor. Their first removal . . . was to be to the house
of a very old friend in Windsor. *E.*xlv.

Wingfield, Mr., an apothecary. Mr. Wingfield most
strenuously recommended it. *E.*xii.

Winthrop, the estate of Mr. Hayter, senior. The estate
at Winthrop is not less than two hundred and fifty
acres, besides the farm near Taunton. *Pers.* ix.

Wolsey, Cardinal. (1) *M.P.* xxxiv. (2) *L. & F.* 31.
(3) " H. of E." in *L. & F.* 88.

Woodcock, Mr. We got her out of the Carriage extremely
well, with only Mr. Woodcock's assistance. *Sand.* ix.

Woodhouse, Emma, younger daughter of Mr. Woodhouse.
Handsome, clever, and rich, with a comfortable home
and happy disposition. *E.*i.

Woodhouse, Henry, father of Emma and Isabella. A
valetudinarian all his life, without activity of mind or
body . . . a much older man in ways than in years.
*E.*i.

Woodhouse, Isabella, his elder daughter, married John Knightley. *See* **Knightley, Isabella.**

Woodston, the parish of which Henry Tilney was incumbent. *N.A.*xx.

Woodville, Elizabeth. Elizabeth Woodville, a Widow, who, poor Woman ! was afterwards confined in a Convent by that Monster of Iniquity and Avarice Henry the 7th. " H. of E." in *L. & F.* 86.

Woolwich. What did Sir Thomas think of Woolwich ? *M.P.*i.

Worcestershire. *Sand.* xii.

Wordsworth. Wordsworth has the true soul of it [poetry]. *Sand.* vii.

Worthing, Sussex. Large overgrown Places, like Brighton and Worthing. *Sand.* i.

Wright, Mrs. Elton's cook. I should be extremely displeased if Wright were to send us up such a dinner. *E.*xxxiii.

Wrotham, Kent, where J.A. spent two days in 1813. *Life,* 291.

Wyards, a small house near Alton, to which Ben Lefroy (*q.v.*) and his wife Anna moved from Hendon in August, 1815. *Life,* 362.

Wynna, Sir John. On Friday we are to be at a private Concert at Sir John Wynna's. " C. of L." in *L. & F.* 103.

Y

Yates, The Hon. John, a friend of Tom Bertram. [He] had not much to recommend him beyond habits of fashion and expense. *M.P.*xii, xiii.

York. (1) *M.P.* xx. (2) I would undertake for five pounds to drive it to York and back again without losing a nail. *N.A.*ix. (3) The family of the poor Man who was hung last assizes at York. *Sand.* xii.

York, The Duke of [of the Wars of the Roses]. " H. of E." in *L. & F.* 86.

Yorkists. *Ibid.* 86.

Yorkshire. (1) Miss Churchill, of a great Yorkshire family. *E.*ii. (2) " Les. C." in *L. & F.* 55.

Younge, Mrs., companion to Georgiana Darcy—" in whose character we were most unhappily deceived." *P.P.* xxxv.

www.ingramcontent.com/pod-product-compliance
Ingram Content Group UK Ltd.
Pitfield, Milton Keynes, MK11 3LW, UK
UKHW042152280225
455719UK00001B/292